MOVE

WHAT THE BODY WANTS

There are many kinds of enchantment. Currently we are enchanted by possessions and speed, gadgets and technology, quick fixes and politicians, the news and crises galore, politics and violence and more. Yet, we long for something beyond all this, something elusive and compelling. Something that will make life magical again. This book offers us a way to explore the biggest, best kept secret of modern times: we have all that is necessary at our fingertips to re-enchant our lives! We don't have to be rich or lucky to crack this secret: all that is required is for us to step back into your skin and move and play in community. Cynthia Winton-Henry and Phil Porter have developed InterPlay to enable us to do just this. Take their book with you into life and you will be rewarded by its accessibility and wisdom. Move is a book for everyone seeking to understand and access the wisdom of their own bodies. It offers us tools, inspiration and encouragement as we share in the grace of living fully in our skins and dance and play spiritually expansive and healing futures into the world. – Marcus Bussey, Senior Lecturer, University of the Sunshine Coast

To be seen, heard and touched by a loving presence; to be creatively witnessed, engaged and accepted wholly, IS What the Body Wants. This powerful, accessible and warm hearted book, is a testimony to inclusive, eclectic friendships, which cross sea, culture, class and race in an attempt to value and create 'art' in the moment. It is an incremental guide to a community practice that places the genius of 'improvisation' at the core of life. – Trish Watts, Singer, Choir Director, Community Arts Developer; President, International Association for Voice Movement Therapy

MOVE

WHAT THE BODY WANTS

FROM THE CREATORS OF
INTERPLAY

Cynthia Winton-Henry
with Phil Porter

WOOD LAKE

Editor: Mike Schwartzentruber
Designer: Robert MacDonald
Proofreader: Patty Berube

Library and Archives Canada Cataloguing in Publication
Winton-Henry, Cynthia
Move : what the body wants / from the creators of Interplay, CynthiaWinton-Henry with Phil Porter.
Previously published under title: What the body wants.
Includes bibliographical references and index.
Issued in print and electronic formats.
ISBN 978-1-77064-915-6 (paperback) – ISBN 978-1-77064-916-3 (html)
1. Mind and body therapies. 2. Self-actualization (Psychology).
I. Porter, Phil, 1953 March 16-, author II. Title. III. Title: What the body wants
RC489.M53W45 2016   615.8'5153   C2016-904311-8   C2016-904312-6

Published by Wood Lake Publishing Inc.
485 Beaver Lake Road, Kelowna, BC, Canada, V4V 1S5
www.woodlakebooks.com | 250.766.2778

Wood Lake Publishing acknowledges the financial support of the Government of Canada through the Canada
Book Fund (CBF) for its publishing activities. Wood Lake Publishing acknowledges the financial support of the
Province of British Columbia through the Book Publishing Tax Credit.

At Wood Lake Publishing, we practice what we publish, being guided by a concern for fairness, justice, and
equal opportunity in all of our relationships with employees and customers. Wood Lake Publishing is committed
to caring for the environment and all creation. Wood Lake Publishing recycles and reuses, and encourages
readers to do the same. Books are printed on 100% post-consumer recycled paper, whenever possible. A
percentage of all profit is donated to charitable organizations.

GOLD

Printing 10 9 8 7 6 5 4 3 2 1
Printed in Canada by Friesens

CONTENTS

WHEN LIFE DRIVES YOU OUT OF YOUR MIND, ENJOY THE RIDE: BODY INTELLECTUALS

WORDS, VOICE, STILLNESS: LET 'EM ALL PLAY

ECSTATIC COMMUNITY: THE GROUP BODY

PLAY THAT HEALS

DANCING LIFE'S DIFFICULT DANCES

For our heart and hearth
Stephen, Katie, and Chinh

———

there is happiness to be had
it hovers in the air waiting
for you to embrace it

let it come in and attach little wings to your heart
so you all can hang out with hope
in the light places

these are challenging days for empaths
turn off the news
be your own best story

LEAH MANN

FOREWORD

AN ETHIC OF PLAY

Somewhere along the road of human development, we managed to shift play from fundamental to peripheral. We think of play as a small subset of activities usually associated with children and childishness. Even my first pictures include the goofy, the silly, the boisterous, and therefore – as an adult with composure – the embarrassing. Cynthia and I have been teaching people to play for oh-so-many years and yet even we share the discomfort of our rooted and sensible cultures with the idea of play.

In fact, play is a much larger set of activities than we first imagine. To play is to do the things that we enjoy, that feed us, that we are compelled to do, that give us deep satisfaction, that lift our spirits, that are fun, that transport us, that are ephemeral, that lead to a sense of accomplishment, or that move us. That covers a wide territory, doesn't it? Look through this lens and you recognize that play is what the body wants. It makes us strong and confident. It makes communities generous and open. It fosters freedom and peace.

Don't we all want more of that?

We have been cut off from play in so many ways. "Get your work done first." "Don't do that!" "How are you going to make a living?" So many voices, even well-meaning ones, have invited, if not compelled, us to restrict our physicality, to pull ourselves in, to be less than we might be. And I am glad that at some point in my life I learned to sit still. But we have been sitting still so much and so long. Our muscles and bones and spirits get quickly creaky.

In the practice of InterPlay and in this book, we invite you to breathe and to move and to tell stories and to sing, but we also suggest that you can find the attitude of play in so many of life's moments. What you consider to be play may be completely different than what I do. And we might surprise each other. I have heard many people describe the meditative satisfaction of washing the dishes or ironing. Some enjoy collating and stapling. When I was a graduate student, I was an assistant manager at a McDonald's. I actually liked counting the French-fry boxes during the Sunday night inventory. Go figure! You may have similarly odd activities that give you secret delight.

In my own life, the world of work and the world of play are intersecting more and more. Since I have so much to do that I can't wait until I get it done to play, I look for an attitude of play in all that I do – the joy, satisfaction, delight, meaning, and engagement that is possible in almost any moment, and I am happier and healthier for it.

I have a secret theory that I will share only with you: I believe that spirituality is actually a subset of play. We have separated out the experiences that lead to depth and meaning and peace from the realm of play and have put them in a completely different territory. In many ways, we have made these experiences into "work" – full of obligation and responsibility. We are so serious about spirituality. Play, despite our preconceptions, leads to depth as well as to lightness. I have experienced it over and over and over again, in my own life and in the lives of those I have played with.

I remember dancing with our friend Sheila at an InterPlay retreat as she coped with her son's AIDs-related illness. During the dance and in the conversations that followed, the whole group of us found ourselves crying and laughing at the same time. It was a holy moment of play.

It isn't hard to reclaim play. But once you do, don't lose it again. Many of the people who are attracted to InterPlay are, like Cynthia and me, over-socialized adults. We don't really risk falling off the wagon of responsibility. You, too, can have more joy, peace, delight, satisfaction, and community. Really, you can. And you will still be able to hold up your corner of the world. It will just be a lot more fun.

PHIL PORTER
InterPlay cofounder

INTRODUCTION

YOU AND THIS BOOK

Move is about reawakening our body wisdom, about saying yes to our whole life, and about being more playful, creative, powerful, and integrated. This is both easy and hard. Lao Tzu says, "All difficult things have their origin in that which is easy, and great things in that which are small." So it is with the seemingly simple ideas and practices in this book. They offer a challenging new way of thinking and behaving, one that is rooted in an ethic of play. One person called this book a conversion process. It may inspire you to play more, to listen to your body more, to redefine spirit and mind, or just to wonder how freedom, play, and being embodied got so hard.

Move is a treasure map and you are the treasure. You need no prior confidence or disposition for your journey. You only need a body and some willingness. As the stories of people in this book reveal, anyone can retrieve the grace, spontaneity, and mystery of interplaying with the ever-dancing universe: aging nuns, prison inmates, scientists, the dying, the depressed, and those with bodies too big, too old, or too artistically trained.

You may want to make reading this book a solo journey. You can also set off on this trip with a companion or supportive group. You may not want to get out of your chair. That is completely acceptable. Even if you just take deep breaths and shake out your body a little every day, you will be doing one of InterPlay's regular exercises. An InterPlay T-shirt says, "Shake Out Whatever You Are Sitting On!" It seems silly, but it works. As you go, I wouldn't be surprised if you got the itch to play in a bigger way.

Based on experience, sharing the *Move* journey with at least one other open-hearted, willing person will speed up positive change and health. It often takes a community body to help individual bodies gain ease. Visit interplay.org for contact with other InterPlayers near you. If you are not ready to be that public, this book is full of companions who began as you have, wandering around looking for something "more." Their stories and voices on the *Like Breathing* downloadable audio resource, offer friendship for those who are returning to the simpler joys of embodied life.

The audio resource, *Like Breathing*, created from nine hours of improvisation, is provided in a downloadable format, to accompany you into the spirit of InterPlay. To listen to or download the *Like Breathing* audio files, go to www.woodlakebooks.com/movemusic and enter the following user name and password. Username: inter Password: play. A complete track list appears on page 319.

Journalling will help you collect insights about your body wisdom as you go. It is surprisingly hard for humans to answer the question, "What do I want?" Brief writings, poems, images, and art can help you track whatever you notice. Body Wisdom is based on noticing the little things in our experience over time. If you find that you cannot write, or if you resist it, that is normal. People have not been trained to integrate their word selves and their moving, singing, being selves. You may need relief from words. Take it. It takes time to get all our parts to easily interplay.

Move is written as a developmental process. One thing builds upon another in the incremental system of teaching InterPlay. Bodies love this incrementality. The mind and spirit like to dash around willy-nilly. But integration is embodied and brings mind, spirit, and heart right together in the present moment. Reweaving our various gifts of thinking, feeling, and action into one symphonic way of being can feel awkward and clumsy. But, in the end, the tapestry is spectacular.

It is also fine to jump around in this book should a particular focus speak to you. Or you might want to take an exercise to a group or meeting to assist others in the step-by-step interplay of becoming more embodied.

My greatest hope is that by reading, noticing, and doing the exercises, you will come to play. That's where the real power is. I am saying a prayer right now that when the time comes to put on the music, or to babble, or sigh out loud, your inner elf will rise up and say, "Ah, what the heck! Time for "elf-awareness!" Or maybe your inner angel will help you out with a nudge. G. K. Chesterton said, "The reason angels can fly is because they take themselves so lightly." In not taking it all too seriously, I hope you will surprise yourself by playing and praying with your four potent embodied gifts: your movement, voice, words, and stillness.

InterPlayers use the processes found in this book over and over. Hand dances; hand-to-hand contact; babbling; "walking, stopping, and running"; deep breaths; and one-breath-at-a-time singing are our ABCs of embodied play. Each practice can lead to more sophisticated play, or suffice as it is to reveal our body wisdom. For instance, a hand dance quickly moves to whole body solo movement.

Once you get going, don't stop. Whatever works for you, keep doing it – even the simplest of things. Whatever doesn't work, let it go. If you are disabled in any way, the key word in InterPlay is "adapt." Take care of yourself and change things to work for you. You know what is best for your own body. What is important is finding the treasure – and the treasure is you.

Move is the fruit of our purposeful desire to change the world and have fun, too. Searching for a way to foster the alive, free, truthful, spontaneous, integrated human beauty and power we've seen when people create, Phil and I listened to our own body wisdom and that of the thousands of people with whom we have played. Encouraged by our friends to find a systematic way to share InterPlay so that they could lead it in their part of the world, we discovered that shared vision, language, common practices, and as much community as you can get, make a huge difference when you want to shift your life toward freedom, playfulness, and becoming more embodied.

I love the fact that it took two people to create InterPlay. Given the word InterPlay, it makes sense that it would. Phil and I are quite different from each other. Although we were both born in Indiana, are strong intuitives, and have a deep commitment to community, creativity, ideas, and embodied teaching, from there we diverge. Phil calls himself the president of fastidious men. He is a *magna cum laude*, well-balanced, even-tempered, methodological thinker who counterbalances my dauntless, messy, bungee-jumping approach to life. His introversion and respect for people's limits counterbalances my tendency to collect herds of gorgeously weird people as friends.

As my co-creator, I give Phil equal credit for this book. Because it doesn't reflect his wonderful humour or clarity, pick up the book he authored called *Having It All: Body, Mind, Heart and Spirit Together Again At Last*. It lays out the philosophy of InterPlay in a highly readable, visionary way.

You may recognize ideas or exercises that seem familiar to you from other systems. For the greater part this is due to coincidence. Phil and I intentionally stayed away from other people's methods. We wanted to develop our own thoughts and practices and discover body wisdom for ourselves. What we share with other teachers and traditions is call for celebration. I am convinced that the universalities found between any two approaches is a testament to the structures guiding the physicality of creation. For instance, I have discovered several people and groups that employ the one-hand dance as a step into the waters of play. The heart of things keeps making itself known to anyone who will listen and can patiently find the simplest forms. To those colleagues who have been researching, rebuilding, and re-teaching the wisdom of the body in this era, I bow down in humble gratitude and acknowledgment. Phil and I consider it a privilege to be among more and more colleagues devoted to rediscovering what our bodies honestly need and want.

———

People ask me, "How did you come to do this?" InterPlay started taking shape for me as a dance major at UCLA in the mid-1970s. In those days, dance and spirit were never used in the same sentence. It seemed completely strange that I had such strong feelings when I danced and sang and played with others, especially in church, but I couldn't help but take my experience seriously. Was I alone? As a person of faith, when I went to college I was pushing up against the hidden force fields of Christianity's anti-dancing bias and academia's spiritless rationality. As a dancer and a young woman with a zeal for expressing her love, I had to ask, "Why, of all the arts, had dance disappeared from the chancel of a world religion that professed the glory of the incarnation and the beauty of creation? And why was physicality and experience so rarely engaged in classrooms?" Rationalism and reason, academia's own brand of piety, appeared dismissive of my basic concerns. Spirit and faith were kept to the back halls of discourse.

One day I asked a professor about dance in the church and she pointed me to Ruth St. Denis' autobiography, *An Unfinished Life*. Thank God for Ruth St. Denis. One of the early 20th-century modern dance pioneers and a teacher to Martha Graham, she had a vision. She called it "The Church of the Divine Dance." As I read about her vision in my L.A. apartment, it literally triggered a mystical experience for me. Immediately, I felt an energy funnel through my head and down my spine. My inner eye opened and I saw everything at once, feeling an intensely personal, yet neutral regard for all living things...no judgment. Everything was completely loved. Flooded with gratitude and only wanting to serve this vision, I felt a call to hold dance and religion together. But how?

I began to seek out places where dancing and religion were still integral to daily life. I found it across the Atlantic Ocean one summer in the village of Taiama, Sierra Leone, West Africa. Whenever drums appeared, dance sprang forth. Even sitting on the side of the road, the drums would come out. An electric, pulsating fire burned deep within the people there.

Back home, Mike Fink, the UCLA campus minister, handed me Margaret Fisk Taylor's book *The Art of the Rhythmic Choir* and bought me a plane ticket to visit Pacific School of Religion in Berkeley, the only interdenominational seminary where dance and religion were taught. There I found professor Doug Adams, an exuberant advocate of dance in the church; Judith Rock, creator of Body and Soul Dance Company; and Phil, my colleague to this day. For ten years in Body and Soul, Judith, Phil, and I choreographed, danced, spoke, wrote, travelled, ate, and pondered questions of body, mind, and faith. We threw our bodies into splits and gaps where people ignored the body, or looked askance at spirit. It was always financially precarious, but unforgettably rewarding.

Seminary led me to ministry. I was ordained on Pentecost Sunday, a day dedicated to tongues of fire and new birth in community. It was a logical step in a life dedicated to grace and spirit. While I do not regret it, pastoring a church was difficult. My irrepressible, playful physicality, sexuality, and the church's needs conflicted. I experienced rejection, ached, and took comfort among others hurt by the church. Still, I knew the church was my base community. It was part of the fabric of my being. It would have been easier to cut off my leg than leave it. So, instead of ostracizing myself to the periphery, I began to claim the dance of life as the prophetic centre of all things, including my tradition. I turned away from a vocation in institutional religion to establish a place in the greater dance of faith. That is when InterPlay really began.

I've discovered that while divine life doesn't require a religion, it needs a sanctuary, someplace to share what our bodies want and need through gracious, hospitable rituals of story, song, movement, and touch. InterPlay is such a place for those who seek freedom to be real, spontaneous, playfully affectionate, and open to truth. I am as surprised as anyone that such a place has arisen like Brigadoon from the mist of the later 20th century. I am as needy of the playful realm of embodied spirit as anyone.

Like everyone else, I wonder at the irony that something as unlikely as play could heal and resurrect people like me. I marvel at how so many unlikely dancers could have so many uncommon transformations – ordinary people, soulfully dancing, singing, and sharing their lives; waltzing across lines of class, gender, religion, sexual orientation, and ethnicity to become a glory-filled, beautiful people again. I have seen nothing work faster or better than the wisdom of the body to bring people home. Nothing in the past. Nothing in the present. And I dare say, nothing in the future. And when things get really bad, the grace in our body only asks to surpass itself. How is that for a miracle cure?

Somebody pinch me. How did I get so lucky? I hope you find some of your own wonder at the wisdom of your body in the pages to come.

INTERPLAY GLOSSARY

Affirmation: to seek out, notice, and name the good in others and the world.

Bodyspirit: the inseparability of body and soul as a condition of our life.

Body data: the bits and pieces of physical information that we notice moment to moment.

Body intellectual: one who pays attention to all forms of physical experience, seeks to be articulate about that information, and uses it as an important basis for understanding the world.

Body knowledge: noticing the patterns of our own body data over time.

Body wisdom: making choices based on our body knowledge for our own good, the good of others, and/or the good of all of creation.

Easy focus: to relax and open up our physical awareness to take in a full range of information.

Focussing: the visual ability to see and notice details, to pay direct attention to one thing at a time.

Exformation: to move information that we have taken into our bodies outward.

Fake dancing: to enthusiastically approximate the quality of a particular movement, style, or activity, even if we are not practiced in it.

Glue people: those who enjoy following others and who create connection and community in the process.

Having: the ability to notice and indulge in our own experience.

Kinesthetic identification: perceiving the movement of others in our own body.

Kinesthetic imagination: using movement to physicalize an intention, to fantasize, or to create realities.

Noticing: the ability to perceive and reflect on our experience.

Physicality of grace: a set of physical experiences describing the satisfying and enlivening state of being calm, centred, energized, alert, relaxed, etc.

Play ethic: in contrast to the work ethic, redefining values based in the physical awareness of creativity, spirituality, ease, and grace.

Spiritual discipline: any physical practice that you undertake to shift patterns, thoughts, and behaviours in order to create something new for your own good or for the good of others.

Stuff, deal, thing: non-specific terms used to describe certain challenging events or experiences, used as an alternative to language that may be loaded or judgmental.

Witnessing: the act of paying attention, enjoying, and taking in the physicality of another person.

WHAT THE BODY WANTS

1

WHAT YOUR
BODY WANTS

Death is a scary word. But here are the words that really, really scare people: *Play. Body. Dance. Feel. Touch.* How do I know? I have taught smart, creative, caring people of all ages, genders, and types for many years. Body wisdom? Yikes! Frankly, it's the same for me. If you want to be taken seriously, which I do, don't say "play, body, dance, feel, or touch."

Meanwhile, men and women of all ages and nationalities sequester me in the shaded corners of my classrooms and confess, "If I could do it all over, I would have danced. I really need to play more, but…"

What do we want? Garrison Keillor, when asked "Do you think all any of us really want, deep down, is to be loved?" said,

No, we want to be rich, to be admired, to eat like a horse and be skinny as a snake. To have small children ask for our autographs, to be on terrific medications that make us calm and witty and sexy. To sing Irving Berlin and Gershwin and Porter at the Oak room and be described in the *Times* as "luminous." But in the absence of all that, it's enough to be loved.

Recently, I asked a graduating Yale student, "What are your peers seeking today?" "Honesty," she said, "and not the Reality TV kind." That rattled me. An ache for honesty. Yes, I want that. But being honest is scary. Spontaneously honest in public? Let someone else be honest first.

Bodies are ruthlessly honest. Play is honest. You can't play unless you are yourself.

We have belittled the body and belittled play. If play is really an innocent, insignificant experience, why do we fear it? It's confusing. We are like Eugene O'Neil who asked, "Why am I afraid to dance, who loves music and rhythm and grace, and song and laughter?" In addition to inheriting traditions suspicious of the body, we judge spontaneous emotion and vulnerability. Being physically playful can make you look too happy, goofy, or, as they say, lead to sex. Embarrassing! Wild abandon is for celebrities who get paid millions. On the opposite end, the media seduces us to emulate the coolly statuesque. Unfortunately, our attempts at "coolness" turn us into wallflowers waiting on the periphery of a wildly infectious, weird, dancing universe.

Phil and I jokingly blame everything restrictive about the body in Western culture on shoulder pads in suits and dresses. Lift your arms up and your suit bunches around your ears. That's not good. Our power costumes keep us standing up straight with our arms at our sides. To this I say, "Bah humbug!" I love TV commercials that show people in suits erupting in joyous dance. To reclaim the body at play is to be a part of a strange revolution, a revolution of personal empowerment and love. To play and fully be ourselves is liberation.

What does your body want? A home, a job, a loving relationship, a community, enough adventure to keep you interested in life? These things are basic. Look deeper and you may
still find the seeds and jewels of secret hopes: the dream of
freedom of speech; the ability to freely create, sing, and love
with abandon. A house, a job, and a marriage provide a secure
framework, but we soon discover that what we really need is
enough affection, time, beauty, play, bigness, loudness, happiness, quietness, space, freedom to tell our truth, and some people to share this with. What does your body want?

———

JOURNAL: SIMPLE WANTS

Notice your senses, emotions, and thoughts. Are there things you
want right now? To lie down? To move? To eat? To be outside? Are
there some simple things you want more of this week, this year?
More quiet, joy, fun? Take a walk today. Instead of focussing on things
difficult to achieve, notice simple ways to fulfill desire. Sing, laugh.

———

Reclaiming body wisdom begins with noticing what creates ease
and joy, and then doing it. It seems so easy. And yet it demands
behaviours that we are no longer accustomed to – being spontaneous, bold, revelatory, and wilder than we are. Jim
Gunshinan, who was then a Catholic priest, surprised himself
when his hymn to the body, *What the Body Wants*, spilled forth.

———

MEDITATION: "WHAT THE BODY WANTS,"
LIKE BREATHING, #20

Read the poem, or – if you prefer, sit back and hear it read to you by
David McCauley.

The body wants to dance.
It wants to get up off the floor and dance.
It wants to get up out of the chair, and dance;
to get from behind the desk and dance;
to get out with people and dance.
The body wants to move.
The body wants to move and touch
and move together with other bodies.
It wants to smell other bodies and taste other bodies.
It wants to be up to its neck in body.
The body wants to be a body.
The body is tired of waiting and resting beneath the mind.
The body falls asleep thinking.
It can't stand the wait between action and action.
It doesn't want to write or call somebody, talk or take a nap.
It wants to move out into the world.
It wants to touch the world of bread and coffee,
soft cloth and rough cloth,
pavement, tree bark, hear car sounds and water sounds.
It wants to tread on things and to feel the weight of things.
It wants to squeeze somebody and be squeezed by somebody.
It wants warmth, sunshine,
breezes and wet sand between its toes.
It wants to jump in water and float.
The body wants to jump off the Golden Gate Bridge.
It wants to fly. It wants to feel with every cell the pull of gravity
and the centrifugal force of turning.
It wants its energy and it wants peace and tranquility.

The body wants to know that it is not alone.
It wants to be big sometimes and small sometimes.
It wants to fit into small safe places and fill up rooms with shouting.
The body wants to vibrate to its own voice
and to feel harmony with other voices and dissonance.
It wants to dance slow and dance fast,
to flow, to thrust, to bend, to be still.
It wants to make beautiful lines and to be seen.
It wants to be fat and skinny, to burst out of its seams.
The body wants everything.
It does not want to be bounded,
but loves to rub, push, and bounce off surfaces.

The body wants to play. In fact, some think the answer to the question, "Will you play with me?" may be more important than the answer to "Do you love me?" Play with me and I know I belong. Our willingness to play tells the truth about our desire to be ourselves with someone. Physical, creative, erotic, and personal, the beauty of play is that no one has to change, no one has to be healed or done with their work to do it. You don't have to play at the same level of intensity or ability. People of all ages, races, abilities, genders, sexualities, histories, gifts, and curses become potential playmates.

In the documentary film *Promises*, Israeli and Palestinian boys who normally threw rocks at each other were given a small chance at friendship. The first question from one boy to the other on the phone was to ask, "Do you want to play?" Later, in games, music, and food they tentatively found each other. Tears of relief followed. Loving our enemies becomes more possible if we first find the smallest ways to play. Watch how quickly children mend the fragile fabric of their relations.

People need to play in ways that are big and little, ways that are safe and not too safe. That is why after work we get on a bike, or go to a gym or a bar to release the pent-up enthusiasm, sexuality, and creativity that we are unable to expend on the job. I have clergy friends who head for a bar with a dance floor after hours at conferences. Their roles dictate restraint, but they are movers and shakers whose bodies, beliefs, and souls are often in conflict.

Elizabeth Lane, a big bodied, intelligent, and caring woman, recognized this as her dilemma in seminary when she decided to listen to what her body wanted.

> The time comes
> To make…
> The temple
> It is a frightening thing to create something
> To step back and let
> Divine
> Seep and flood
> And pour forth
> Through what you've made.
> It isn't always a safe thing
> People have gotten in trouble for doing this sort of thing…
> And it doesn't seem to get any easier…
> But to be alive
> No, that's too small a word
> We can be alive without it…
> The heartbeat is the last to go
> It tries so hard to remind us.
>
> But to take this life
> This opportunity
> Not take it for granted
> Take it for all it's worth

Wring every bit of bliss out of it
One must try.

The goodness of embodiment happens in this moment and this moment alone. It looks more like play than work and you won't have to change yourself. It will be scary in an awesome way, because the best things in life, the things we really, really want make us feel more vulnerable. That's the problem and that's the fun.

―――

MEDITATION: "BODY PRAYER,"
LIKE BREATHING, #1

Listen to Curran Reichert sing "Body Prayer." Curran is a spiritual director and former musical theatre professional. In her improvisation, she sees your body as a mystery – beloved and perfect. Notice your openness or resistance to the notion that you, your body, and your love are wanted.

―――

"WHEN I FIRST SAW AN INTERPLAY CLASS IN ACTION...
I JUST DID NOT WANT ANY PART OF IT ... HAD THEY GONE
MAD? WOMEN PLAYING?"

BARBARA WALSH

a Roman Catholic Sister, leads InterPlay at Grace Center in San
Francisco a residential program for women in recovery.

There is a group of very special women with whom I have the
privilege to work each day. They have voluntarily come together
to live in a small, unique residential setting and to engage in a
12-step program in order to gain their recovery from various
addictions. Many of them have been told over and over, "You
are worthless. You are nothing. Hopeless. Ugly. You're a junkie,
a drunk, etc. etc. Even if you try, you will never make it. You
cannot change. You are trash." People have used them and they
have been cast aside. Not wanted, they have imbibed from bot-
tles, drowned in drugs, gotten hooked on sex, pills, and more.

One afternoon, we introduced them to InterPlay ... to dancing their dance and telling their story. To playing in community. It was simple ... profound ... moving ... touching ... spiritual ... incarnational. Maree said, "When I first saw an InterPlay
class in action...I just did not want any part of it...had they
gone mad? Grown women actually playing? But I went, and do
you know it was at Interplay that my happy little girl came to
life after being buried for 30 years. My sad little girl goes to the
therapy classes, but my happy little girl comes to InterPlay. I
need both!"

Regina said, "At first I thought I cannot dance. I never have.
Do they really expect me to dance!? But then I heard the laugh-

ter from the heart. I went. I danced and danced just the way I wanted to. I had become a free bird and no one criticized, laughed, or even commented! I am a dancer!"

Gwen said, "After years of abuse of all kinds, I had become paranoid about touch – being touched or touching others. At InterPlay I learned the beauty, the wonder of touch. It was gentle and musical! There were no strings attached! This wonderful expression was mine. I had reclaimed touch."

Anna said, "In order to support my addiction, I had danced for others, for money, etc. But in InterPlay I can dance by myself for myself...no leering eyes to stare at me...no drunken hands to touch me. I am the Dance! I learned to dance for myself."

And finally, Pat said, "At last there were people who were interested, actually interested in my story. I do not think I had even told it to myself! My imagination has been released! In turn, I was able to hear the story behind other people's lives. Respect and love seemed to just float around the room...How great it was to laugh, to laugh with others. People laughed with each other not at each other."

The women came to experience in their whole being a release of tension. And, at a deeper level, to feel the release of resentments and hurts. They felt their anger, owned it, and let it go! They have watched with awe and respect their sisters in recovery discover their own unique preciousness and beauty. They have learned to give to one another, not only through words but in spirit through dance movement. They have relaxed in an atmosphere of acceptance and gentleness. Through storytelling they have listened to each other. For many of them, they have been listened to for the first time as their story has been told. Community has grown. They have laughed together...with honesty and real joy!

The jewel in this sparkling crown is that when the women dance the 12 steps of AA into their bodies, they receive them into their very being: 1. We admitted we were powerless over alcohol and drugs, that our lives had become unmanageable; 2. We came to believe that a power greater than our selves could restore us to sanity. And on and on with the remaining steps.

The other night as they sat in a circle, they thanked me for all I'd done. They said how they loved the little girl in me who would suddenly appear in the room as she kicked off her shoes. Then they gave me a beautiful gift – a sculpture of a circle of dancers! Wow! To dance and play with these women at Grace Center is my delight, my privilege, and I would not trade it for anything.

2

THE OPPOSITE OF STRESS

Have you ever experienced stress?" I ask people. Like a bad joke, that question will evoke laughter and loud groans everywhere, from Goshen, Indiana; to Waga Waga, Australia. Who am I kidding?

JOURNAL: STRESS AND ITS OPPOSITE
Write down three or four physical sensations you have when you are in stress. Now remember a physical experience you've had that was the opposite of stress. What was that like in your body? List the good physical sensations.

The opposite of stress! When I ask people to remember when they have experienced the opposite of stress, I love to watch their faces change. A smile of relief comes as eyes close and shoulders drop. With ready answers they recall physical sensations like "open, energized, peaceful, laughing, connected." I tell them, "In InterPlay, we call these sensations grace, the physicality of grace. Just as you can identify stress and what causes it, you can recognize the experience of grace and choose more of the things that create it."

Grace is such a wonderful word. An attribute of dancers, grace comes from the Latin, and it means "favour, esteem, kindness, pleasing, and agreeable." It's all about thanksgiving, gratitude before meals, physical ease and beauty, hospitality, and divine blessing. According to poets, both animals and trees can have grace. A theological definition of the word comes 14th in the list of definitions, where in some cases it seems to have been infected by one of those pesky religious bugs that eats away at perfectly wonderful phenomena. In the Christian tradition, you might hear expressions such as, "though I am unworthy of your grace, Oh God...," or "grace is a gift, undeserved." To me, this made grace seem like a giant lotto game. What a gamble. Buy the right ticket, go to the right vendor, and God's grace might land in your lap – maybe. Grace didn't seem to befall a person if they went looking for it. I hated that. What did a person need to do in order to have more grace?

On the other hand, in an ancient apocryphal text found in the Apocryphal Acts of John called the "Hymn of Jesus," Jesus sings to his dancing disciples, "Grace dances, dance ye all."

Artists, dancers, singers, poets, and athletes often invoke the muses of grace and beauty as they struggle with obstacles and impossible feats. From the beginning, I longed to be one of these athletes of spirit. Still, I've often been stuck in troubles and challenges, toiling and toiling and toiling against things that interrupted grace. Unwittingly, I have physically conjured up more challenge in the process.

It is surprisingly easy to overlook things that offer the physicality of grace: music, dance, stillness, nature, making love, art, gardening, singing, being with those I love, pets, getting organized, creating with and for others, and really playing; all in favour of focussing on problems. Had I known early on what I know now, I might not have worked so hard to find grace or to solve all my problems and to heal all the wounds I discovered in myself. Now I know that grace is nature's intention for us. Instead of being elusive, grace infuses life; it is intrinsic to every organism in its natural order, including our own. Dom Helder Camera, a beloved musician, bishop, and champion for liberation, wrote in *Questions for Living*,

God has stamped a rhythm in human beings, animals, plants, and even stones. A person walking, a bird flying, a leaf falling – everything proclaims the beginning of a dance. At the heart of the atom, in the ballet of the stars, rhythm and harmony have been sown by our Creator! Listening to music, watching dance – these are true prayers!

Sri Ramakrishna said, "The winds of grace are always blowing, but we must raise our sails." In order to catch the experience of grace in our body, one trick is to slow down, to go the speed of the body, and to notice what specifically creates grace for you. Then do and have these things as fully and regularly as you can. Ila Leavy, in her 60s, shows us the way in her poem *Grrrr*.

Grrrr
Sounds like growling
Till we add the ACE, the One.
Maybe make it a spade
So we can lift hands,
arms up, out,
then to a point-of-breathe deeply-prayer.
A rainbow-flashed
in sprinkler water along Smith's ditch

Just today on my way
To walk the flower beds.
A fiesta triangle of zinnias
Made me the girl planting
Seeds, I still tend gardens
Though they're mostly inside of me!

Last night I gathered
The half-cycled moon riding
Out the colour change of
Blues and clouds,
the glide Of trombone variation of
"Blue Bells, Scotland," as leaves
On high branches danced
In the same slight breeze
That lifted a few gray hairs.

Gr-ACE visits more often
Now and it rarely
growls.

Breathing deeply, prayer, walking among flower beds, tending gardens, aging with ease, colour, and the feel of the outdoor breeze: these are Ila's grace-makers. Paying attention to her body, noticing what creates grace in the moment (as well as what brings stress), and then choosing to do these things, Ila increases grace by being in her body outdoors, where zinnias and bluebells regularly lift her.

The physicality of grace is the cornerstone of a joyous, dancing life. If you notice what tends to bring you grace, you can choose these things more often. Would it make a difference in the world if you had more grace and less stress? Choosing grace is body wisdom.

JOURNAL: HELLO GRACE

Notice any sensations you enjoy in this moment. Expand the moment to include the day or the week. Say hello to these sensations. They are often there, but go unnoticed.

———

Sometimes we need to pay attention to the whole of our physical experience in order to sense goodness. Instead of focussing on the challenging feelings in your experience, can you sense an overall energy, hopefulness, grounding, or other experience that you enjoy? We call this "body data," noticing bits and pieces of physical information in the moment. At this moment, late afternoon pours in over my right shoulder. My spine is erect and although I am fatigued from an active day, I feel engaged and enthusiastic about this manuscript.

———

JOURNAL: GETTING TO KNOW YOUR GRACE

Write down or share with someone the things that repeatedly bring you joy or peace, or that bring aliveness to your body. Name people, places, or activities that most consistently create grace for you. They are your grace-makers. Are you around them enough? How might have you recently made grace for others? Now write down or share things that don't create grace for you.

———

Seeking out and surrounding myself with grace-makers makes it possible for me to physically give back to the world. We all have grace heroes, beacons of love and action that have made a remarkable difference in the world: people like Dorothy Day; Mother Teresa; Cesar Chavez, Gandhi; Ella Fitzgerald; Martin Luther King, Jr.; Thich Nhat Hahn; and the Dali Llama. But there are unsung heroes all around us, too. They encircle us as dancing saints, the movers and shakers who marched, sat, loved, served, spoke, and sang out loud. They lead the way and show us what it's like to be passionate, and to live simply and fully, even in the extremes of life.

JOURNAL: GETTING GRACE-MAKERS

Write down those people who have helped you experience the physicality of grace in the last few days, weeks, or years. You may not know their name. Honour them by thanking or celebrating them in some way. Doing this, you celebrate the good that is in you.

Your body knowledge is arrived at by noticing the patterns in your body data over time. When you actively choose to create grace for yourself, or for others, grace spills over and creates more. Actively choosing our body's grace is body wisdom. Body wisdom is the process of using the bits and pieces of body data in the moment, noticing their patterns over time, and from this, making choices to create good for ourselves, for others, or for all of creation.

If we believe that the divine is in everything, including each of us, then it is possible to see humans as sources of grace, at any time and in any situation. Grace-making falters only when we force specific forms of grace onto others: "You must dance!" "You need to laugh more!" "You should get out and be with people." "You need to make more money!" That's when we get into trouble. Forced grace is an oxymoron. Freedom to be filled by what moves us is grace's trademark. However, such freedom is demanding. It is a big step to be the one making sure we get enough grace for ourselves.

Several years ago I met a man, a Presbyterian elder in his 60s, at an annual, week-long sacred dance workshop. Slowed by polio, psoriasis, and a multitude of afflictions, he continued to show up every year to dance. He sought things that gave him joy and peace. A true disciple of the mystery of grace, he told me that grace cured his polio at age four, kept him from dying in 1954 when he had a ruptured appendix, stopped the growth of malignant bladder tumors in 1983, and enabled him to survive and tell about being struck by a car in a crosswalk. Something is definitely on his side. He never lost his holy innocence. He hangs out with loving people, is not overly concerned with other's reactions, and is the most unselfconscious, openhearted person I know. Every year that I see him, I can't help thinking, "This man dances. It makes a difference and he knows it."

It often seems to me that people in the worst circumstances are the ones who are most ready to dance, play, or do whatever it takes. As Adam Houschild says, "Once in a while one meets people who have crossed an invisible line, stepping into a territory from which there is no turning back; they are already in such trouble that nothing they say will make it any better, they are relaxed and open and they laugh."

This book is full of such folk. Those of us who are in full swing, working hard, and are busy, busy, busy, need other reasons to choose grace. My favour is that I know how contagious stress is. Being around someone in stress is the worst. If that's what it's like to be around me when I am in stress, Lord, let me choose grace!

As a person who hopes to contribute to changing the world for the better, I have to pay attention to what creates grace for my body, for my community, and for the earth. Grace is as physically contagious as stress. When you live your grace physically, others get it from you.

The physicality of grace is a kind of body wisdom compass. If you want to be wise, have integrity, joy, and do good, then do just as a wise man said: "Love your neighbour as your-self." As one prone to workaholism, self-righteousness, and bouts of protective rage, I am not the queen of play as some see me. I am definitely a disciple of play, though. Horrified that my home is a place where I have been known to dance and play the least, I created InterPlay in order to give my best self, not only to the world, but to my family as well.

PARTNER: DIFFERENCES BETWEEN MY BODY'S GRACE AND YOURS

Ask a friend or someone you live with about their sleep pattern. What creates the best sleep for them? Ask them to be detailed. When do they like to go to bed? Hour many hours of sleep do they need to get a good night's rest? Then share your body wisdom about sleep. Compare the two of you. Honour the differences.

Different things create grace for different people. My middle-school daughter told me recently, "Mom, when you wake me up in the morning, please don't rub my arm lightly and say in that singy voice, 'Honnnnneyyyyy, it's time to wake uhhhhupppp.' I hate that. Just shake me a little and say, 'Katie, it's time to wake up.'" I laughed and remembered that I, too, had felt irritated by my mother's morning voice. My daughter likes direct, firm energy to help her transition from sleep. Better yet, if she can, she prefers to wake up on her own. The fastest way to help people to grace is to listen to and affirm their body wisdom.

Each body has a unique way of moving and being. It is like you are your own small country, with a distinct, unique ethnic dance. You are not meant to move like anybody else and are under no obligation to dance anyone else's dance. Diversity is inherent in each of us. Body structure, stories, traumas, developmental timing, urges, and energetic needs vary dramatically from person to person. Though we inherit physical traits from our families and communities, many of us know that we don't even fit within our own cultures. There are behaviours in other cultures and families that suit us better.

I had a Caucasian student whose mother and father loved living and working with Native American peoples. However, the slower pace drove my student crazy. She needed more challenge, more stimulation. Not until she could really listen to her own body did she realize her parent's body wisdom was unique and so was her own. Though she appreciated her Native American experience, she needed other ways and another lifestyle to create and have her grace. She no longer had to judge others in order to affirm her own way of being.

I haven't found a person without physical oddities. I joke with Phil that he is the only normal person I know, the sole person present at meetings for adult children of normal parents. Ask him how he's doing and he's always fine. He's a perfectly happy stoic. He's also a wildly creative, introverted, Hoosier living in a construction project in Oakland. For a living, he leads a band of unlikely dancers into the world. Normal? No one is normal. Phil is fiercely gifted. This makes him unusual. His differences could isolate him, but they don't because he knows how to play in the world. He is honest, self-revelatory, and amused at life.

To love the body for what it wants, to encourage each body toward its grace, is a challenge to our beliefs, pictures, and tightly-held values. Thousands of images and ideas tell us what it is to be happy and whole. Yet pictures don't go deep enough. Neither do words. As a student of the life of Jesus of Nazareth, I am fascinated by his ability to enact embodied grace beyond religious and social expectations. His life purpose – "I came that they may have life and have it in abundance" (John 10:10) – guided him to see grace in each person and to help give form to that grace. With women, he had honest rabbinical conversations. Grace. With the crippled, he restored physical capacity. Grace. With those who had lost their way, he said, follow me. Grace. All of these transactions were rooted in a physicality of grace. Something physical happened.

We make love too much of a mystery. Love is the open invitation to be who we are at our greatest and most human. Grace is not dependent on stature, flexibility, intelligence, or training. It is just there, accessible in every moment. The key is to listen to what your body wants. If I let myself go, here is what I want.

I want goofy play to put shiny light on everyone centre stage
to shoot us through the trap door into our real love lives.
I want common sense to be destiny's golden field
all treasures dug up and out for free on the lawn.
I want to swing, swing, swing, monkey crazy
from the great tree of life's branches so
happy hospitable, its fruit drops down
constant and easy to feed us, even
pain when not too rotten. I want
to make an offering to the god
of innocence that you cannot
have me back until I lick
life like a red hot. Not
only do I want all this
I got it. Ask me
what I want.
I'll tell you.
Grace.

"I WAS TAKEN UP INTO A LARGER WORLD THAN I HAD
KNOWN BEFORE, SOMETHING BIG AND INFINITELY GENTLE
AND MYSTERIOUS AND AT THE SAME TIME I WAS ALL
THERE AND FELT GROUNDED."

JIM GUNSHINAN

trained as an artificial heart engineer and then a priest
until depression, anxiety, and love taught him to dance
and speak his truth.

Father John Dunne, one of my seminary professors at the University of Notre Dame, told a story in class about a man who walked up a mountain looking for God. Halfway up the mountain he passed someone going the other way. It was God, coming down the mountain, toward the human community, where there is "love and war." By the time I took John's class, I was working on my second master's degree – the first one was in bioengineering. Before getting into the Master of Divinity program, I needed to take a year of philosophy classes. Altogether, I had been in higher education of one sort or another from 1977 until the year I took John's class in 1988. So when I was ordained a Catholic priest in April 1989, I was very ready to begin a long trip down the mountain – from an academic life, to ministry, and toward an embodied spirituality.

I worked as an associate pastor in a South Bend, Indiana, parish for four years, and then became a campus minister at Saint Mary's College, a small Catholic liberal arts college for women, also in South Bend. In the fall of my fifth year at Saint Mary's, a friend and dance teacher at the college, Indi Deickgrafe, asked me to go with her to a dance workshop in

Richmond, Indiana, a day's drive from Saint Mary's, at the Earlham School of Religion. Indi and her student Caroline had studied with Cynthia Winton-Henry and Phil Porter the previous summer in California, and they loved InterPlay. The idea of going to a dance workshop felt awkward, because I was a priest, and celibate, and dancing was a near occasion of sin for a celibate man – too close to sex to be safe. But I wanted to dance.

I had been an athlete in college and a runner after that, until I developed back problems. I missed the feeling of my body in motion. And I had a crush on Indi. So I said I'd go.

During a break on Saturday afternoon, many of the workshop participants, mostly men and women ministers or seminary students from Protestant denominations, lay flat on the wooden dance floor among gym bags and sweatshirts. I lay there with my face resting on my two hands and my elbows splayed out. Indi laid her cheek in the crook of my elbow, making a pillow out of it. (I can still close my eyes and feel the warmth of her face on the skin of my arm.)

On the last day of the workshop, I did an improvised dance with Caroline. Caroline took my hand and led me around the dance floor, weaving her way through the other dancers. There might have been music playing, but I don't remember it. What I do remember is that we separated, and I rushed to a corner of the room. I was afraid of what I was feeling because it was so different than thinking. I had spent most of my life thinking. I dropped to the floor and curled into a ball, with one arm reaching out in a plaintive gesture. Caroline, who has strong arms and muscular legs, took hold of my hand and pulled me back into the dance. I wonder if this is what evangelical Christians who are born-again experience? I felt, for as long as the dance lasted, like a whole person. I was taken up into a larger world than I had known before, something big and infinitely gentle and mysterious and at the same time I was all there and felt grounded.

A few days after the workshop, back in South Bend, I took a walk by the Saint Joseph River. It was a clear sunny day at the very end of September. I started my walk with a blissful feeling of wholeness and well-being left over from the dance workshop. But as I passed between the AM General building on one side, and a branch of the river on the other, my heart began to race. I was suddenly out of breath, and I felt terrified – as if the ground had dropped out from underneath me and I was left hanging in the air without support. I went from feeling the euphoria of the dance with Caroline in Richmond to feeling panic. My life was bound by vows I had taken and by the expectations of the church, and by fear of giving up a life that felt secure.

The anxiety stayed. Often, I would wake up at 3 a.m. in a panic – several long, slow, deep breaths calmed me down. After three months of lack of sleep and an inability to focus on my work as a campus minister, I took a medical leave from Saint Mary's. I spent several weeks flying around the country to be someplace where I felt safe (even though I was terrified to fly). I spent three weeks at Apple Farm, a retreat centre in Michigan. I spent a few weeks with a favourite aunt and uncle in South Bend, a week in California with a good friend, and two weeks in Maryland with my father. But I couldn't shake the anxiety. I was frustrated and fell in and out of hopeless, agitated depression.

I wanted to begin work again during the second semester at the college, but after a week back in South Bend I realized I still couldn't focus enough on liturgy preparation, preaching, or my other duties as a campus minister. From my office at the college, I called Father Carl Eby, the head of my religious order, the Congregation of Holy Cross, and asked for help. I wept when he told me that the community would do whatever it took to get me happy and healthy again. When he told me about a centre in Saint Louis for priests and religious brothers in psychological trouble, I said I would go.

At Saint Michael's Community, a ministry begun by a recovering alcoholic priest, I was given individual counselling and group counselling. Yoga, Tai Chi, and morning dance aerobics were options, and I did all three. I was dancing again and it was such a relief. We painted, wrote down, and acted out feelings we had habitually repressed as a result of our religious training – "Father" is always in control of his emotions – and lifelong habits begun in childhood. I was in treatment with alcoholic and drug-addicted priests and religious brothers, and a few men charged with the sexual abuse of children. Many of the men were in the process of coming out as gay and deciding if they could stay working for a church that condemns the way they love.

I cried a lot at Saint Michael's. All I had to do was put on some music and start to move, alone in my room, and the tears would flow. When I left Saint Michael's, I had instructions from my therapist and spiritual director there to "continue integrating your sexuality and spirituality using art as a medium." This wasn't a recommendation to leave a celibate priesthood, but to live artfully as a sexual being capable of emotional intimacy in prayer, in chaste friendships with men and women, and through ministry and creativity. I had met priests, both in the seminary and at St. Michael's, for whom prayer, celibate friendships, and creative ministry were enough. I asked Carl for a year in Berkeley, near the Graduate Theological Union there, where Holy Cross has a house for priests on sabbatical. Carl had earlier promised me a sabbatical and we agreed that the treatment centre didn't count.

Knowing that I wanted to continue dancing, but being ambivalent about what this would mean, I called Cynthia to ask about InterPlay classes in the Bay Area. She told me that she had been carrying around a poem of mine for a year, one I had read and danced to at the workshop in Indiana. She said that, after my experience in Richmond, she figured we would meet again. I was already penciled in for a whole series of InterPlay classes in Oakland, where the program is centred. The poem is called *Impossible Angle*, and it's about a series of sculptures done by a Croatian sculptor, Anton Mestrovich. It depicts Abraham, Sarah, Jacob, Mary, the mother of Jesus, and other characters from the Bible, their stone faces looking up, level with the sky, their necks at an impossible angle. The poem, like the sculpture, expressed the deep tension I felt between what I knew (how to love as a celibate man) and what I had – a body longing for physical intimacy.

When I arrived in Berkeley, I had a choice between going on a retreat in Los Angeles with some other priests, and participating in a dance workshop with Cynthia and Phil at Isis Oasis, a retreat centre near Napa Valley. Dedicated to the Egyptian goddess, Isis Oasis is a place where clothing is optional at the pool and in the hot tub. It took all my courage to turn my car north on I-80 toward Isis and not south on I-5 toward LA.

I did my first contact improvisation at Isis Oasis with Cynthia. It's a form of dance where two people make body contact, hold it for a moment, and then move in whatever way their bodies feel like moving. I did a lot of rubbing, pushing, pulling, embracing, and running away from Cynthia and the other dancers. I felt the delicious sensuality of body contact and also, still, the fear of it. Once I watched two dancers come together in a shape so beautiful – one dancer leaning on another – that I stopped breathing for a moment and then started to cry. I soaked naked in a hot tub every night. "You're a priest? That's interesting," said someone sitting across from me through the steam. "I'm thinking about it," I said.

I thought about it for a year while dancing, writing poetry, and doing Yoga. At the end of my sabbatical year, I was accepted to the Squaw Valley Community of Writers, an annual poetry workshop that is also known as poetry boot camp. There I met poets who were also, in a fundamental way, priests, ministers of the Word, who connect people to themselves and the world around them through the articulation of shared experiences. Only the poet's priesthood uses the whole body and all the senses to make those connections. The poet's priesthood, like the dancer's, is not confined to ritual, preaching from a pulpit, and hearing confessions.

After the Squaw Valley Community of Writers, I finished my sabbatical as I began it, with an InterPlay workshop at Isis, and went to work with a friend and fellow priest at Andre House, in Oakland, a halfway house for men in recovery from addictions. On April 1, 1999, exactly ten years from the day of my ordination as a priest, on my way to hear Marie Howe, a favourite poet, read poems from her book *What the Living Do*, I dropped a letter of resignation from my religious community into a mailbox on the corner of LeRoy and Virginia streets in Berkeley. Later, I began a long process, called laicization, much like an annulment, asking the Vatican to release me from the priesthood and to allow me to marry in the Catholic Church.

In the first year after leaving the priesthood, I had shingles; a nightmare where I said "no" to the Pope, who was pleading with me to be a priest again; and one where I argued about my decision with my 95-year-old grandmother, who was born and raised among the rocks and hills of Calabria, in Southern Italy, and who ranks way ahead of the Pope in my family's hierarchy. She scared me more than the Pope does, because I feared her disapproval more. And she hadn't approved of my leaving the priesthood. People of her generation were taught that a priest in the family guaranteed heaven for the parents and grandparents. She kept asking me during my first few years out of the priesthood when I was going to become a priest again. "You are a smart boy. You could have been a bishop," she said.

It's been five years, and I've come a long way down the mountain. I got a job at Black Oak Books in Berkeley selling books and introducing speakers for the bookstore's reading series. I took editing classes at night and eventually landed a job at Home Energy, a magazine that covers energy-efficient residential construction. I haven't received a decision from the Vatican about my petition for laicization, but I'm not waiting. I'm engaged to be married and we are planning on having at least one child, although we're both now in our mid-40s. I'll ask for the church's blessing later, when and if the laicization comes through. The Catholic Church has lots of rules about sex and marriage, but also always keeps the back door open for those of us who fall short of the ideal moral life.

My fiancée, Michele, is a scientist, who, like me, spent many years in school, and who, like me, hasn't felt ready for marriage until now. My love for Michele is intimate and physical and spiritual and sometimes I want to scream, I feel so tied to her and so tied to aspects of myself that I'd rather escape from – such as my tendency to want to crawl into the fetal position when I am threatened by powerful emotions. It's not Caroline now, but Michele who sometimes pulls me out of my isolation. She is patient with me, but also insists that I be honest with her emotionally. When I can admit to her my fears, they dissipate; my world expands again and love is given and received. I never thought physical pleasure was important before, not when I was busy trying to earn the love of those around me by working hard and being good. Pleasure still seems a little decadent, but the more we give each other pleasure out of love, the less decadent it feels and the more it feels like love.

The last time I saw my grandmother dance was at her 50th wedding anniversary celebration. Several months ago, she asked me not when am I going to become a priest again, but when am I going to get married. She died shortly after asking, having almost made it to the end of her 100th year. She changed, right up to the end of her life, and I feel inspired that I can too – change, and love, and suffer, and arrive at the end into the arms of a loving God. Then we'll all dance.

3

RISKING INTERPLAY

The plagues of modern society linger too close – disease, depression, relationship anxiety, job dissatisfaction, and cultural shame. Perhaps you are an expert at stress or, if you aren't the expert, those around you are. You want your life back or wonder if you ever had one at all. Somehow you are guessing that you need to listen more to your body.

You walk into an InterPlay class. What trouble have you gotten yourself into now? Somebody suggested InterPlay, but said it's hard to describe because it's a place where everything comes together and there are no words for that. It's like trying to describe Buddhism or how to ride a bicycle. "It's just something you have to experience," they said. The light in their eyes seemed strangely convincing. Besides, you were looking for something. What was it?

The next thing you know the InterPlay leader invites everyone to take a deep breath. In and out. Again, a deep breath, with a Friday night kind of sigh. The room bursts with a surprisingly big exhale and spontaneous laughter erupts. There's a funny relief in it all. Things aren't so serious. Everyone sighs out loud again. Next, the leader asks everyone to shake out one of their hands, then the other. Feet get shook, butts shake, even voices shake. It's like taking laundry out of a basket, shaking and hanging it on the line to sun dry. Talk about loosening up! This is definitely silly. Still, it's pretty easy and everyone seems to do it. The leader invites everyone to massage their face and head for a few seconds. Then another deep breath. So far so good. The leader seems easy and yes, embodied. Nobody seems too worried about how to do these things. There are no mirrors. No left feet or right feet. Just feet.

"The one rule in InterPlay," the leader says, "is take care of yourself. I can't do that for you. So please adapt anything we do to fit your own body. It's even okay to sit or lie down. If you feel like you need to watch that's fine. We consider witnessing a form of participation."

Just like the shaking and breathing, you continue following along, doing things that are easy and somehow fun. You are squirming, stretching, opening your arms wide, and popping out of your everydayness a little. You are encouraged to shake out the day and to let your troubles roll off your shoulders as you bend over. Everyone has joined in. You physically open your arms outstretched and then close your arms around yourself like a hug. There's more laughter as the leader tells everyone to move their hips in a circle, joking about how hips are the centre of creation so we might as well move them for a change. Next thing you know, arms are swinging, flinging, and thrusting. There is 20 seconds of fake tap-dancing while everyone looks surprisingly like they know what they're doing. What better way to "tap" into the spirituality of delight? After things calm down again, everyone is invited to do slow smooth movements, a kind of fake Tai Chi. Who would have thought that this kind of easy moving could feel so good? Even after a short time, you feel better.

Before you know it, you are into other things, all of which seem to feel both loosening but strangely profound. The group is invited to walk around the room. This turns out to be more fun than you'd think. When you walk backwards for a few seconds, the leader encourages everyone to say "thank you" if you run into someone. Pretty soon, it's almost as if a choreographed dance is arising. There are initial feelings of self-consciousness and curiosity about this way of being with others.

The leader moves people into pairs. "We're going to do a little babbling." You sit down with someone near you. "Talk to your partner for 30 seconds about hair," smiles the leader. Hesitantly, you begin. Words start to flow and sputter forth with less concern than usual. Words become playthings, each partner playing for a brief moment with ideas and words that the leader offers. You get to know several people through their brief stories and musings, and have opportunities to notice what it's like to do this. The leader listens to people's reflections and seems affirming. Somebody remarks that it was easier to do than they thought.

Later, you are partnered with someone hand-to-hand. After a little pushing and pulling and experimenting with what two hands can do, what appears to be a wild form of advanced hand shaking feels more like prayer than prayer. You take another deep breath, look around, and realize that you might like these people. Maybe Plato was right when he said, "You can discover more about a person in an hour of play than in a lifetime of conversation."

There doesn't seem to be any right or wrong way to do things. People are encouraged to notice the obvious. You notice that you're still trying to figure out if there are more rules here. Both the leader and participants share insights. It's wonderful that an activity so physical can also include ideas, observations about energy and spirit, and odd bits of life that are often overlooked. In the end, the group stands in a circle and sings a simple improvised song. It sounds beautiful and no one seems to want to leave. How did that happen?

———

InterPlay helps people embody their lives through their own words and stories, movement, stillness, and voice. These four human expressions are four doors into wisdom. Each way reveals a unique aspect of our wisdom and spirit. To interplay with these areas with others in community, even though it is a risk to do so, inspires unparalleled wisdom and grace for those who are willing. The changes that take place through InterPlay's simple activities are astonishing. Unlikely dancers emerge from their challenging lives and can't believe themselves. Perhaps it is because InterPlay starts with the body. When our bodies really feel included, alive in community, and are affirmed, without having to explain everything, then grace and fun follow. It's not that hard to do, but at first it seems impossible. Stepping over our initial self-consciousness feels like leaping the Great Wall of China. In hindsight, we see it is more the size of a speed bump.

Once your body is having grace and remembering how to get it, people discover that celebrating in community is incredibly powerful. As a people, we learn embodied ways of witnessing and affirming, and find ourselves mysteriously reconnecting to the dance of life. Eventually, our whole selves want to get in on the act. Each one of us retrieves the way that we like to move, talk, voice, and love. We re-find our self. We become a celebrant of the unstoppable dance of life, and feel as free as a child, while maintaining wisdom and maturity.

For those who InterPlay, their way back into a playful life, a simple blueprint reveals itself: practices and ideas that begin with bodies bring thought, feeling, and spirit back into harmony. The first and most difficult step is always walking onto the grace floor. After that, the door swings wide open into a life that is sexier, sillier, more profound, and oddly, feels closer to God.

MEDITATION: "OPEN THE DOOR,"
***LIKE BREATHING*, #17**

Listen to "Open the Door," a bluesy, irreverent invitation to reunion and life. Are there sides of you that might have taken a hike and that need to be seduced back? Can you keep your sense of humour about this? Can this reunion be fun?

"I RAN TOWARD THEM AND HURLED MYSELF INTO THEIR ARMS."

JEANETTE STOKES

an energetic, spiritual teacher, discovered that she
had to risk in order to find self-care.

It was a Friday night at the Church of Reconciliation, in Chapel Hill, the first time I performed with Off the Deep End Performance Ensemble. Everything was improvised. I knew I had to get out there, so I walked to the centre of the space waving my hand over my head, hollering, "My turn, my turn," and introduced myself saying, "I'm an extrovert. They said I could go early in the show. I just read Sam Keen's *Learning to Fly*. He's the philosopher and theologian who wrote *To a Dancing God* in the 1960s. A few years ago, at the tender age of 62, Sam took up trapeze. A local circus school was offering trapeze classes for lay people. He signed up, fell in love with flying, and eventually bought his own trapeze rig. With the rig set up on his farm in Sonoma County, he formed a program called Upward Bound. We don't have a trapeze rig set up in the church, but I'm going to demonstrate the next best thing."

Then, I asked for help from four strong male colleagues. The four men stood close together on one side of the dance floor and I ran toward them and hurled myself into their arms. I did it three times. The last time, one man caught me and swung me around and around. I felt like I was flying. I loved it.

On the back jacket of Sam Keen's book, Clarissa Pinkola Estes praises him and applauds his "freedom from stagnating fears, which can be attained by leaping towards the strong and outstretched arms of one's deepest desires." When I dance, I sometimes feel like that is what I'm doing. I feel it again when I paint. It is a feeling I'm trying to have more of in my life, launching myself in the direction of my deep desires, instead of always in the direction of what I think I ought to be doing. It scares me. It usually makes me feel like I'm being irresponsible.

Sam Keen talks about becoming a connoisseur of fear. I like that. Instead of moving away from things that scare me, like a new trick on the trapeze, I can move toward it, being careful, more or less, preparing carefully before attempting something a little beyond my skill level.

When I'm really honest, I have to say that there are a lot of things in life that scare me. I don't just mean the big things like death, violence, and running out of money, all of which nearly scare the life out of me. I mean the normal things, like being honest with a friend about my feelings, painting when I really want to paint, and spending more time by myself. I have opportunities every single day to run across my fears, to feel my fears, and to leap towards the outstretched arms of my deepest desires. I get to choose whether to run the vacuum cleaner or to paint. And oddly, I find that the more I paint and dance, the happier I am.

EASY BODY,
EASY SOUL

4

FINDING YOUR EASY BODY

People take me aside to confess frustrations and fears about their body. Many say, "Even if I wanted to be in my body, I've been in my head too long." Their eyebrows are furrowed. Their chest is caved. Everything seems like work.

One of the great shortcuts to the physicality of grace is easy focus. Easy focus is the experience of the physical state of openness throughout our being. This chapter shows you how to have easy focus and an easier body.

Though we blame headiness for the experience of being out of balance, we may have just overworked our eyes. A lifetime of reading words, looking at computer screens, watching out, and observing detailed information with analytical visual focus, literally pulls our primary awareness to the centre of our forehead and eyes. Sympathetically, our body sense follows as we narrow our focus. We tighten our range of movement. People call this behaviour thinking or being in their head, because that's where they feel themselves to be. Phil and I call this being in your "focuser."

The good news is that analysis and thought needn't occur only in tight, limited ways. Thinking can include physically opening your mind to include all aspects of your physical experience. If you want to open your wisdom, creativity, and insight, open up your body. The expression "it's easier than you think" is literally true. Dancers, athletes, artists, scientists, and explorers can "think" with their whole being.

PRACTICE: SQUINCH YOUR EYES INTO SHARP FOCUS
Look at an object. Notice the precise details. Give the object a good hard look. Exaggerate and squinch your brow. Notice accompanying feelings in the rest of your body. Now lighten your expression, but keep the hard focus. This is how we may have been taught to look at things.

Though there is nothing wrong with focussing behaviour, over time our bodies fatigue. This is true whenever we repeat an activity over and over. Eventually, the body rebels. Rewarded for staying focussed and maintaining serious outlooks, many people grow weary beyond words and become desperate for alternative ways of being. Vacations and free time aren't enough. We need things that don't require so much effort.

PRACTICE: HAVE YOUR EASY FOCUS
Give your face a rub. Close your eyes. Massage the place between your eyes. Take a deep breath. When you relax, softly open your eyes with an easy focus. Take in the whole scene. Enjoy being fed by the whole of what you see, rather than by analyzing or looking at one thing and the next.

Desiring to have more grace and ease, Phil and I developed InterPlay practices that led us to a sense of whole-body ease. They are so simple and accessible they seem silly. They don't require much money, time, sophisticated technique, or piles of experience. And they bring immediate results. They are as easy as shaking your arms and taking a deep breath. Rather than trying to not think, not feel, or not act, you are invited to have your whole self. The following practices are part of every warm up we do with people. They can be done either standing or sitting.

PRACTICE: SHAKE IT OUT

Shake out one hand. Shake out the other hand. Shake a foot. Shake the other foot. Shake out whatever you are sitting on, or get up and shake your hips. Shake out your middle. Shake out your voice. If you are laughing, that is the best shaking of all. Shaking is a fast way to release muscle tension and redistribute body awareness.

PRACTICE: LET IT OUT WITH A SIGH

At the very beginning of the *Like Breathing* audio resource, listen to the sigh. Now, take your own deep breath and let it out with a sigh. Sigh like it's Friday. Do it again. Breathing and sighing is a lifesaver. Sighing is like an inner vibrator. It loosens up the insides.

PRACTICE: STRETCH, SQUIRM, AND POP OUT OF YOUR SKIN

Stretch your arms over your head, then out to the sides – take up all the space you need by popping out of the envelope of your skin. Be really big for a second.

PRACTICE: MINI-MASSAGE

Give your face a mini-massage. Rub your scalp, ears, and jaw. Massage the middle of your forehead and eyes to help relax your focuser.

PRACTICE: GAZE

Close your eyes. As you open them, let your gaze be easy, taking in the view as if you were watching a sunset or a campfire.

JOURNAL: SAVOUR AND REFLECT

Take a little time to notice and reflect on how you feel after you shake yourself out, and take a deep breath or massage your face for 15 seconds. Savouring these good sensations is something we can do to have more awareness of grace. In InterPlay, we like to say, "Savour, savour, savour." We already know how to pay attention to the icky stuff.

Easy focus creates easier bodies and a more whole-body approach to seeing and knowing. It's how we operate in unselfconscious play where shape, gender, weight, flexibility, IQ, talents, ethnicity, cultural experience, metabolism, and limitations aren't something to get over or even look at; they just simply are. There is a kind of self-forgetfulness in the easy-focus quality of our experience. In fact, ease in the body feels so good and peaceful, it is more like a non-feeling. You may not notice your general sense of openness and wellness.

Your language may also indirectly affect your sense of ease and wholeness. It is common, for instance, for us to say, "I have a body." The image of "having a body" suggests that our bodies are something apart from who we are, something we may possess, run, or own. "Having a body" implies that we are other than our flesh, a notion that has been reinforced by religious teaching that the soul is over and above our bodies. But we do more than merely occupy skin. The body is not a stopping-off place. It is a destination for soulful living. Body and soul are one. Human life is meant to be soulfully lived. This is a physical reality. Acting as if we don't belong in our body doesn't change the fact that we are attached to it. If we are over-attached to our physical desires, this is an even better reason to practice easy focus, to lighten, but not to give up on our sense of integration.

Claiming, celebrating, and being at peace in our body is our quest. No matter if you have a birthmark on your face, a disease that makes you shake, a speech impediment, a photographic memory, a genius that awkwardly sets you apart, horrific memories that shut parts of you away, so much sensitivity that you are unbearably withdrawn, or you feel so average that no one notices you – your exact physicality is you. Embracing your *bodymindheartspirit* creates grace and power. Resisting or diminishing you takes energy.

Being your body is not an impediment to spirituality, creativity, maturity, reason, thought, relationship, or community. Quite the opposite. It is how to really have it all. You cannot laugh, cry, analyze, or imagine without your wondrous body. Emotions, language, voice, and speech are physicalities. Even intellect is physical. Human thoughts are physical dances that involve our entire being, not just isolated areas of the brain. We always think in body. What is more, I've discovered that when I move or create, whole new thoughts occur. Wide, easy access to all of our experience escalates our capacity to perceive and to know. No wonder people's lives become wiser, bigger, and more wonderful in the process.

———

JOURNAL: MY BODY IS ME

On paper, list ten parts of your body. Include parts you rarely consider or see. To the right of each body part, write one to three words of description in a positive way. Maybe even with an easy focus (for example: leg – strong, recovering, hairy). Take your paper and fold back the list of body parts so that you see only adjectives. Say aloud "I am" in front of each set of descriptions: "I am strong, recovering, hairy." Reflect on these statements.

———

We are our bodies in this precise moment. Whatever our truth, our physicality is good. It is possible to create more ease even around our greatest vulnerabilities. As Henri Nouwen, a great spiritual teacher, once wrote, "What we experience as complete failure is the essence of our spiritual healing…at the center of the failure is joy, the dance."

———

"I HAVE EVOLVED FROM MOSTLY LIVING OUT OF MY HEAD SPACE TO LIVING FROM MY HEART AND GUTS."

———

ANNE BAILEY

When Anne Bailey, a talented office manager, developed severe vision problems requiring surgery, she needed to rely more on her whole body to think and see.

I used to live out of my head space, but now I live more from my heart and guts. Recently, with four others, we got together for a night of play. What a night this turned out to be. So much happened for each of us. In particular, two people had been dancing, and then my friend, Rae, just let the CD of music continue. With just a wink (no words) she invited me to join her. The words sung by Trisha Watts were, "Come, rest and wait in the wilderness. Listen and see with your heart." In that dance, I felt again the importance of seeing and listening with my heart. My eye-sight can be critical and judgmental. I need to practice the softer, gentler, more accepting heart-sight more often. Being witnessed in this dance was so powerful, so nurturing.

How did this happen? Like most things in my life, this has been a slow and gradual becoming. I have an affinity with numbers, math, shapes. The steps I take are small; the growth I make is measured, but the Spirit is spontaneous and together we make dances. Dancing and living from my heart, I have had to be led and taught by others. Even today I am slow to move or respond. So it was, the first time I met Cynthia and Phil. Everyone had paired off, and that left me with Phil. I wanted to run from the room! Not wanting to draw attention to myself, I resisted the urge to flee. My recent work was in the area of Catholic health care and one of the values of this organization is human dignity. It's difficult to describe what that means, but for me it means never feeling less-than, or making someone else feel less-than. It is a call to be greater. That is what I experienced in that first hand-dance with Phil. What he was able to communicate to me non-verbally was an affirmation of my self-worth and dignity, which has remained with me to this day, building my confidence bit by bit.

Still, it was hard. One night, Phil asked for three solo dancers to dance before the rest of the group. I looked down, not wanting to meet Phil's gaze, for I knew he would pick me. He did anyway. He said to remember to use the whole space. So when he looked up from finding a track on the CD, I was using the space behind the pillar and the grand piano!

The reality of what a huge step it was for me to do that dance in full view of the group hit me about 15 minutes later and I cried. But later, at our closing celebration, Suellen was dancing a blessing for each individual. She picked up something from each person's character, either a gift they already possessed or one they wished they could possess. When she came to me, she wordlessly invited me to join her. I responded and just as we started to dance together, she snuck into my place and motioned that the floor was mine to have on my own. It now seems to me that we do not become something until others call it forth or draw it out of us. Remembering that enabling moment still brings tears to my eyes today…a huge step on the journey of becoming a dancing spirit!

The most fulfilling dance of my life happened when we were invited to dance, in front of one other person, how we were right now. I had just had two days and nights so full of stuff, it's a wonder my head hadn't exploded: feelings of dark and light, heaviness and lightness, burden and freedom, insecurity and affirmation, hesitancy and blessing. I had journeyed deep within and had just begun to sort out these threads and to make some sense of them. Dancing, with Suellen as my witness, I was aware of the light coming through the stained glass windows and I played with shape, shadow, and stillness. When I finished, I felt no need to talk about the confusion of emotions I'd been going through the previous few days; my dance had expressed it all. My dance was my vocabulary, my sounding board, my sense-maker. And the response of my witness? "That was unspeakably beautiful, sacred, Divine."

When I reflect on it now, it all seems so natural. Recently, on a weekend away for personal development, each person was asked to write down what we noticed about each other. At the top of the list people gave me were extraordinary words – singer and dancer! Then, courageous, with a sense of humour. A practical soul who is fun. Soft and strong, like a cherry. Patient, gentle, willing to listen, mischievous, fun-loving, full of surprises. I am a paradox!

5

BODYSPIRIT REUNION

Driving is one of the ways that some of us activate our daydreamy, easy focus. We are alert, open, and ideas seem to come with less effort. It has been while driving on the freeway that I have received some of my greatest insights. Like the time I suddenly realized that having an opportunity to be a creature, and even to feel pain, is a privilege longed for by all things unborn. This caused me to wonder. What if being born is the ultimate goal of all of creation and we spend all of our time complaining about it? What if the difficulty we encounter in life is the labour of a greater birth?

Rather than dismiss physical matter as "less than" spirit, I propose we think of spirit and matter as one lovable union. "The soul loves the body," said the 12th-century mystic Meister Eckhardt. It is good to be born into this body. What's more, when there is no hierarchy of spirit over body, we can embrace material life's joy and suffering as a great spiritual honour. As

Irenaeus, an early Christian theologian, wrote, "The glory of God is a human being fully alive."

Instead of the myth that sees only spirit as infinite and big, the fact is, your body may be as big as your spirit. Our senses extend around the globe and connect us to the great beyond. Our bodies do not stop at our skin. There is more to physicality and human physics than that. Light waves bounce off our retinas and connect us to the farthest stars. Unheard sound waves affect us. The pull of the moon affects us. We affect everything as well. This affect is our physical interconnection. Our body is big.

PRACTICE: EXPAND BEYOND YOUR SKIN

Sense the space you take up. Is it a lot of space or just a little? Open your arms out wide. Sense your bigger body.

PRACTICE: SENSE DISTANT CONNECTIONS

Imagine someone you know far away. Can you physically feel your connection to them in your body? You know you are connected through a felt sense. It may be so subtle that you never thought of it as a physical feeling. Notice your connection to light and sound. Listen and see things beyond you.

JOURNAL: THE SIZE OF YOUR BODYSPIRIT

Can you think of yourself as a big body? What comes to you as you expand the idea of your body to match your picture of spirit?

Physicality is basic to all of our experience, including that which we consider spiritual. Spirit is not just a little part of us. It is as big as we are.

An important first step in reuniting body and soul is to become aware of how we talk about these concepts. Language powerfully shapes our behaviours. For instance, the women's movement taught that using exclusive male terms limits our collective imagination as to what women can do and where they can go. Likewise, repeatedly using the words body, mind, heart, and spirit, reinforces the notion that they are separate from one another. These categories may have at one time helped to nuance our understanding of human experience, but today, Phil and I believe that they hold us back from experiencing integration. (See our book *Having It All: Body Mind Heart and Spirit Together Again At Last*, Wing It! Press, 1997.)

Language is physical. It is embodied in form and effect. Our body organizes itself to kinesthetically reflect every image and idea we hold. Today, many people use affirmations to change self-image and to influence their course of action. The words we tell ourselves, or are told, are powerful. Verbal abuse is physical abuse. It affects our bodies. Language is inseparable from our experience.

The term "bodyspirit" shifts our language to reflect integration. Bodyspirit reminds us that body and soul are one and need to be treated as such. Would it make a difference if every person who struck or harmed another knew that they were damaging spirit or soul?

People involved in the movement to reintegrate body, mind, heart, and spirit are seeking a word to express this integration. Many use the word "bodymind." Similar to the split between body and soul, when we think of the word, mind, we tend to reference our head. Yet the brain and five senses connect to the whole body. Mind is in the whole. Referencing our head as mind, we too easily get stuck in behaviours that limit intellect and cognitive imagination.

Split language affects us. Hanneke Jansen is a Dutch research scientist living in the United States. She attends a Protestant church, speaks several languages fluently, has an inquisitive loving spirit, and knows that dance, creativity, and colour are elemental to her spirituality and intellect. What community can embrace her wholeness? Dancing in the lab, talking physics in church, speaking Dutch in her adopted country, being known as loving by more than her partner – all of these would be considered unusual behaviours. This is a communal loss. Intuition tells me that Hanneke's ability to dance and imagine is related to her search for a cure for cancer. But how will we ever know? By limiting a person, we limit his or her contribution, wisdom, and power for good. Who knows? We may be preventing someone from discovering a cure for cancer by limiting their behaviours. The Einsteins of the world have uncovered groundbreaking hypotheses through accident, dreams, visions, and intuition.

Language that separates the body away from spirit makes the body small, the spirit small, and the mind too small. Separated out, we send each part to a separate locality to have its needs met: gyms for the body, church-synagogue-temple for spirit, schools and business for the mind, marriage and romance for the heart. And yet we think through our difficult decisions at the gym, have spiritual experiences while reading a book, fall in love at church, and have many intelligent conversations with a mate.

Each of us is a universe of paradoxes. Unlikely realities coexist in us at once. Being enthusiastically and utterly embodied in a world that insists on segregating physicality leads us to realize how few places exist that allow us to be all of who we are. This is why in InterPlay we find grace in the idea that physicality is basic. We are big bodies. Our mind, heart, and spirit are one size – the size of our biggest, wildest, most beautiful body. Beyond the limits of skin, reaching as far as the farthest star or coming in as close as a baby in our arms, physicality is an expanding, contracting, flexible reality. We are one magical thing: mysterious, vast, tiny microcosms in the biggest body of all.

All efforts to know who we are are worthy and illuminating, but finally impossible. We are an unfolding, evolving universe. We are life, movement, rest. We are creators of offspring we cannot control. We are even death. To dance this dance of life is to take hold of all of this mystery, have it, and love it. When we do this, oh, what a reunion it is.

MEDITATION: "MY HEART IS OPEN,"
***LIKE BREATHING*, #3**

Listen to "My Heart Is Open." Trisha Watts' improvisation sings us into a spacious wholeness that embraces our bodies and the greater body of the world.

"MY LIFE IS LIKE A PICTURE PUZZLE WITH PIECES THAT
DON'T SEEM TO FIT."

———

CHUCK SELNER

a 60-something, retired non-profit executive, grandpa, and
minister living with AIDS, was shocked when grace carried him
over the threshold of a new life.

Sometimes I think my life is like a picture puzzle with pieces that don't seem to fit. Like being a father, grandfather, gay, a minister, and a recovering alcoholic with AIDS. Five years ago I was a 150-pound weakling…barely able to crawl out of bed or to walk my dog, Sunny. I wondered if I would hang around much longer. After my partner Geoffrey died, I purchased a smaller apartment and thought it would soon be my turn.

Everyone knows about suffering to some degree, but coping with it is another matter. I remember my first AIDS-related hospital stay. I fully expected to die.

Angry at having to quit work, I remember staring at the orange juice carton on my tray table. Alone in the enforced isolation of my room, I suddenly said out loud, "I ordered apple juice!" My arm moved. My patience and understanding broke with a splash all over the floor. Feeling embarrassed, I called the nursing station to have it cleaned up before someone could slip and fall. As the nurse quietly wiped up the floor, I decided I needed to explain my frustrations to her. She encouraged me to also talk to my regular doctor. Her patient understanding reminded me that there is a place for a range of feelings. I now realize that my anger motivated me to listen to my body.

My body felt exhausted! Returning home, I had to have help walking Sunny. I soon began to push myself so I would not have to ask for help. After the first few weeks, though, I learned that people feel good when invited to help out. My dog was my first birthday gift from Geoffrey. The first words that we knew Sunny could understand were "Dance, Sunny! Dance!" – which he did to get a treat.

About this time, my good friend Phil Porter called from California. He was coming to Chicago to lead a workshop at the Cultural Center. I went to the workshop where I found myself partnered with a man named Lowell. He began to move with more energy than I could handle. Growing tired, I remembered Phil saying to "go your own pace" and thought to myself, "It's really amazing to move this much. Maybe God is pulling me through." Remembering my recent Yoga class, I dropped into a child's pose with my eyes closed, to find a place of rest and to seek inner stillness; "a good spiritual practice" it is said. Suddenly, I felt myself being lifted by strong hands on my wrists. I was behind Lowell and I had to struggle to stand on my feet when he pulled me forward up through his legs and brought me to standing with my arms spread-eagled. I felt in my whole body, "God has pulled me through."

There is wisdom in my body. Now when I dance to the Gloria Gaynor disco beat of "I Will Survive," like I do when I perform, I mean it with my whole body. Though I still get easily winded from energetic dancing, I understand the need for complimentary physical therapies and I include InterPlay: dance, storytelling, singing, and stillness as spiritual practice. I also found a local HIV / AIDS community group that offers full-body massage, acupuncture, and chiropractic. When I was told my medications inflated my cholesterol readings, I began to work out at a gym! I started to sing with the Community Renewal Chorus, a mission arm of the churches in Chicago. I went with them on a tour of Eastern Europe. At Auschwitz, I saw the pink triangles of the gay people who died there. I began to volunteer in more places and I helped push the United Church AIDS Network to hold the first United Church of Christ retreat for people with AIDS.

Even as I celebrate the gifts of life, I sometimes complain of fatigue or other ailments. One day I complained to my psychiatrist, who treats me for AIDS-related depression. I told him, "I don't have as much energy as I would like." The doctor responded, "Well, you're not exactly a spring chicken!" His sly reverse and perverse psychology worked. That summer I actually did a spring chicken dance at a retreat, moved into a bigger apartment, and started taking modern-dance classes from a teacher older in years than I am. I've even performed a solo in one of her dance concerts and now have a one man show called *Dancing by Heart.*

Now, looking at the cup of life that is mine, I learn to look in the midst of challenges for the potential of healing, grace, and even love. This is God's transformation. To dance by heart has given me the freedom to be public with all of me. I can enjoy being me: a man, a minister, a gay man living with AIDS, a recovering alcoholic, a father, a grandfather, and most of all, a simple human being. We're never too old to dance!

6

REAWAKEN YOUR SPIRIT DANCE

Instead of running errands, one day I decided to dance them. Suddenly, my world flooded with sensations of grace and ease. I was awake, bigger. My steps didn't change. My task didn't change. Nothing was different except my smile. Or was it? Thich Nhat Hahn, who teaches simple walking prayer, calls this peace. I call it the dance of life.

Allowing yourself to think and feel like a dancer can create extraordinary shifts in your everyday realities. Psychologist Gay Hendricks knows this well enough to say, "There are fools who dance and fools who watch the dance. If I must be a fool, let me be a dancing fool."

I've seen it again and again. In a worship service, I watched a famous African-American preacher move up and down the chancel steps, breathing and gesturing with his whole being. No pulpit could contain him. After the service I greeted him saying, "I'm a dancer too." He laughed and nodded knowingly. Four-year-old Marissa, when asked to throw away her trash, jumped up, garbage held aloft like an Olympic torch, and ran toward the barrel with a long, loud whoop. Her task became an ecstatic song and dance. Flipping through channels on television, I observed an Asian man sitting on a boulder in a stream. He moved his arms through the air as if in prayer. In that moment, he inhabited a different world from me. So did 60-year-old Charlene, when I saw her dance a prayer for a partner. She grew radiant as her arms lifted and she fell with ease to her arthritic knees. Afterwards, she couldn't believe her knees didn't hurt.

It is a completely new thing for many adults to let their own movement take the lead. Movement has a mind of its own. The risk lies in opening to the spirit of dance right where you are. Though it's a psychic leap, you can do it sitting in a chair. Dancing won't kill you, but everything will feel oddly at stake. You are likely to become a little bigger, bolder, and clearer about who you are. You may feel like you'll lose your mind a little and you are almost certain to have more fun.

You are movement. It's not just something we do. It's who we are. Nothing can stop that, not even death. In his book *Perelandra*, C. S. Lewis writes,

The Great Dance does not wait to be perfect until the peoples of the Low Worlds are gathered into it. We speak not of when it will begin. It has begun from before always. There is no time when we did not rejoice before [his] face as now. The dance which we dance is at the centre and for the dance all things are made!

Saying yes to ourselves as movement can be as simple as seeing the world in movement. Yet for so many it is incredibly difficult to imagine dancing this life. Not until we get a push from dire circumstance, have a desperate need for healing, or a haunting sense that something important is missing, do we get onto the dance floor of life. That's why I consider those who have begun to play – even tentatively – advanced human beings. In my experience, advanced human beings are those who are willing to cast off social expectation and to say YES to being a body and to dancing their life.

———

JOURNAL: SENSE THE WORLD'S DANCE

Close your eyes. Imagine yourself dancing. What do you notice? Now, look out your window. Take a deep breath. Using easy focus, observe the world's motion. What do you notice?

———

If you can feel yourself dancing even while you are still, then you are tapping into your kinesthetic imagination. Kinesthesia is the name for our sense of movement. Kinesthetic imagination is our ability to create subtle or symbolic experiences in our muscles, breath, and imagery. You've heard of how athletes imagine themselves to perform perfectly. Their images communicate directly with their muscles.

Different from mundane living, igniting our kinesthetic imagination is like awakening from sleep. When the dancer in you wakes up, you feel greater wholeness, like grace is multiplying through every cell.

———

PRACTICE AND JOURNAL: HELLO KINESTHETIC IMAGINATION

Imagine standing on a mountain with your outstretched arms touching the sky. Or imagine that you are holding someone you love. Notice your physical sensations (feelings, breath, muscle tension, body memory).

———

Your body's sympathetic nervous system says you are doing what you imagine. A napping dog moans and twitches as it dreams. A mother's catastrophic thought translates immediately into shallow breath and tight muscles. Meditation, affirmations, guided imagery, and prayer affect our mood, body, and can bring healing.

———

PLAY: FREEING ONE ARM: "KOKOPELE,"
LIKE BREATHING, #4

Raise an arm in the air and for 30 seconds move it smoothly through the space around you. Feel the space around you. Rather than direct your arm, let it move freely. This is more like surfing than driving a car. Now, let your arm form a shape. Move from shape to shape like a sculptor. Enjoy each stillness. Play between flow and shapes, according to the desire and energy in your body.

Select "Kokopele," #4 from *Like Breathing*, played by Stan Stewart and Amar Khalsa. In Pueblo Indian mythology, Kokopele was a master magician whose humpback was actually a bundle of sacred objects. Adorned in bright red Macaw feathers and bathed in the Eternal Flame of passion and creativity, he mesmerized observers with his flute and body as he swayed in front of the communal fire. Kokopele reminded people of a time before Creation, when each person was a spark from the Great Mystery's Eternal Flame that had fallen to earth to seed the Mother with fertile thoughts, ideas, and actions.

Kokopele carries the spirit of renewal. Perhaps he will help you as you play this music and let your arm lead. If you feel bored or judgmental, move in a way that is more challenging or interesting. Or simply rest. Don't push yourself to "feel the dance." You may dance best when you are completely still, arms resting in quiet. If you feel resistant to moving, however, you may only have the hurdle of inertia in your way. Physics says that a body at rest remains at rest. It may take a small act of will to begin to move. But once you do, you can experience the rewarding, simple joy of moving.

JOURNAL: REFLECT

Notice thoughts, images, feelings, words, memories, or sensations. A poem may come, or something that you did not expect. Welcome anything that comes. Forget about being a body. Just an image or memory may be what your body offers.

Momentum, energy, flow, and power are always at play. They have more meaning in our life than we ordinarily acknowledge. By moving, we gain access to information that cannot be gained any other way. Our moving body senses the field of relationships, both visible and invisible, imaginary and material, a "virtual realm of power" according to philosopher Suzanne Langer. To let your mind and body join together in the dance, to dance for the sheer enjoyment of moving, or to dance as a way to pray is, for many of us, to experience spirit more quickly and naturally. And if you don't know if you can call the sensations you feel spirit, perhaps it's enough to claim what Germaine Greer did when she said, "The essence of pleasure is spontaneity."

Young children inhabit this way of being more than adults do. They pretend to be a deer and forget they are a human. We needn't cast aside the child's way of seeing and experiencing. Artists and mystics keep hold of it. Kinesthetic imagination is a powerful ally. Anything that you can embody and embrace with imagination and joy, you can create ten times more quickly. The ability to pretend in whole-bodied ways is a missing link in adult practices. I predict that, in the future, many more of us will use movement and other forms of imagining to uncover solutions to life questions: scientific, business, political, religious, and personal.

"I WAS WORKING TO SAVE THE WORLD ... BUT I DID NOT DANCE."

JO LIN

a father, caregiver, and activist, has come to know that
Tai Chi connects him to his Asian ancestry, his garden
connects him to the earth, singing connects him to spirit,
and dancing connects him to life.

My father came to Australia from Swatow / Shantou in southern China in 1937. He returned to China in 1945 to marry my mother, to whom he had been betrothed. They settled in Australia, where they had two sons and two daughters. I am number two son, number three child. We are a close family and keep in touch with our large clan, who have mostly settled in Sydney.

We grew up as *Teo Chiu*-speaking children in a big, run-down house in an English-speaking suburban neighbourhood. Aware of our differences, we were not always understanding or accepting of them. When I had a Surfie or Beetle haircut, I thought I looked like the other boys at school. I wanted to belong so much that I tried to throw away my first language and culture, especially what family means. Added to a conservative Chinese upbringing were some conservative Baptist teenage years. No dancing.

Perhaps always feeling on the margins of Australian society, I first studied to be a social worker. I wanted to change the lives of the poor and disadvantaged as Jesus did. This vision extended to the wider world when Australia became involved in the American War in Vietnam. When I opposed this involvement and compulsory military service, my activism began and I left the church.

I met my life partner, Ellie, in 1974 in Adelaide. She had just returned to Australia after some years living and working in England. Before that she was a teacher on an aboriginal settlement in central Australia. During the 1970s, we and our friends worked collectively, lived communally, and acted globally and locally! Love and activism. I was working to save the world…but I did not dance.

In 1979, we returned to Sydney to be closer to both sets of parents. We shared the parenting of our two daughters and I began to speak our dialect again, and to work in the family retailing and wholesaling business. I also began to learn and practice Tai Chi. We saw that the world continued to be unfair for many people. So we continued to work for aboriginal land rights, women's rights, gay rights, global justice in food and agriculture, independence for East Timor and West Papua, a nuclear free and independent Pacific, and a healthy and sustainable planet. No small task! I still did not dance.

Playing with, caring for, and learning from our daughters was the most wonderful, life-enriching experience. Bronwyn and Joanna grew up in rural New South Wales and in multicultural Sydney with their Chinese, Anglo-Celtic-European, and Tongan extended family. They learned to dance the suburban way with an encouraging Cecchetti ballet teacher. They did jazz and I enjoyed looking on. Meanwhile, I continued to practice Tai Chi every day, even when I was working on agricultural projects in remote areas of Australia and South East Asia.

About five years ago, Ellie's sister Fiona came to Sydney to take part in a conference that linked spirituality with creative writing, the visual arts, and movement. At the end of the conference, we watched a final movement presentation. I turned to Ellie and said, "One day I'm going to do that."

A year later, I tentatively enrolled for an InterPlay experience in Sydney. I fell in love with InterPlay. Each day that week I woke up at 4:00 a.m. in excited anticipation. I began by practicing Tai Chi under a star-filled sky – a wonderful summer experience before the mozzies (mosquitoes) came out. This was followed by InterPlay. What a combination! From the first day, I knew I could become a dancer!

Phil, Cynthia, and other friends in Sydney have added many gifts to my journey of dance and life: the art of inclusion, the practice of "staying in" when I/we feel like running away, trust in my intuition, and an openness to share with others. The intimacy of holding and being held in dance is life-giving for me. I treasure the moments of stillness just before moving off together, the sensing of each other, the waiting, the trusting, the surges of energy, the mutuality. These are beyond words.

I have also begun to move beyond words in other areas. In my activist work, I used to facilitate social/structural analysis workshops based on an action-reflection model. This approach has been used in the struggle for justice in many countries. Even though we would incorporate drama, visual arts, and music into parts of the process, it was still very much word-based. Movement emphasizes mutuality. This mutuality breaks down the "them and us" separation, which is often present in activist and solidarity work.

InterPlay and other dance/movement approaches have given me skills and confidence to be with people, to hold them in my hands and in my heart in a different way, to accept persons as they are in that moment, and to allow a physical connection of love and support with them to develop. For me, this is a different way of working for a more just world.

WHAT IF THE HOKEY POKEY REALLY IS WHAT IT'S ALL ABOUT?

7

GIVE YOURSELF
A HAND

I have to admit it. I have a picture in my head of grace dressed in a pink tutu doing little footsy steps across the floor, her arms elegantly but stiffly poised. Just like the picture of God as a man with a gray beard on a throne, this image has got to go. Instead of trying so hard to be perfect, or despairing that we ever will be, grace happens more often when "Life" opens the backyard gate, nudges us out, and teasingly asks, "Hey, what's out here?" Always a little uncertain, we wobble wide-eyed into a wondrous world and fall more in love with it.

If you want more grace, you've got to surprise yourself. Abandon your pictures of a perfectly-posed graceful being. Try moving in a jerky manner. Exploding the images of good and bad ways to move, talk, or be, is more fun than trying to be a serious dancer of life. You can drop 100 pounds of heaviness in a split second. You don't even have to get over feeling strange. Feeling awkward is a hallmark of humility, humour, and humanity, all having to do with humus – being earthy, or of the earth.

———

PLAY: SMOOTH AND JERKY: "WALK STOP RUN," *LIKE BREATHING*, #5

Ever feel like a jerk? I do. Life has jerky and smooth moments. You can dance it all. Raise an arm in the air and let it move smoothly through the space. Then for just ten seconds each, move your arm in different ways: move smooth and fast; move your arm in a jerky way; move your arm jerky and slow. Now interplay with the two dynamics of smooth and jerky. As you move, you may want to meditate on the bumps and breaths of your day. Sometimes you will move in rhythm to the music. Sometimes you will move in contrast to it. Both are fine. There is no right way to do this dance. Any dance can be a meditation, prayer, or a mini-vacation.

———

When your hand dances, your whole body is dancing. A Zen koan asks, "What is the sound of one hand clapping?" I think it is the simple sound of one hand dancing. Think for a minute about how we talk about hands: hands on, hand out, hand it over, handiwork, handyman, handler, shake hands, put your hands up, hand-me-down. Throughout our lives, our hands are dancing, making things, connecting us, feeding us, and precisely shaping space.

To dance with one arm requires little room, energy, or experience. It's as if our hands and arms have been dancing all along, but we hadn't noticed. Watch. People communicate with hands in a language parallel to their speech. It's communication that cannot be put into words, yet it conveys a world of meaning. A world Confucius inferred when he said, "What I hear I forget, what I see I remember, what I do I know." This world of embodied knowing is the world of our bodyspirits.

All it takes is one arm-dance to open up a world. Nancy Brink, an InterPlayer, muses about this in her poem *That Hand*.

That Hand
would have been enough –
held my interest
as it lay quietly, at first,
then began to tap
that unintentional rhythm
on the back of the chair
on the back of my shoulder
on the back of my neck
on the back of my head
climbed to the top
and took off,
that hand
would have been enough.

Barbara Nixon taught hand dancing to eight middle-school youth at a church camp in the Oregon mountains, including to an 11-year-old boy who was finally able to break free from his anxiety-filled, perfection-driven life. Barbara watched and he brought her to tears when he danced and played. She said, "He had never done it before. He kept saying, "I wish my life was like this." Now others are working with him to ensure he gets the help he needs to have the life he desires." How many of us are waiting for this life?

To enter fully into life takes practice. Unfortunately, it doesn't happen magically. This is why we play when we are kids and why we must play now. Play builds competency at a manageable level of risk. And it's fun. To change your life, change your practice. If you really want to change, make change fun. Dance with all of the dynamics of life. Then when the forsaken and disjointed side of life inevitably appears, you can do more than react. You will have physical choices that you have practiced. Who knows? Maybe you will even see the hard times as part of the dance, and dance them. We are discovering that if your body can dance, you can more easily find your truth. If you can dance, your body feels more ease. An easy body is an incredibly good thing to cultivate and to have access to in the hard times.

Dancing with contrasting dynamics gives us a way to more joyfully practice embodying our choices. Any dance can be a mini-ritual, whether it is improvised or rehearsed. It creates a space, a container for playing with choices, even tough ones. In addition to moving in ways you like to move, you can familiarize yourself with icky, demented, overwhelmingly powerful, intense, and weird aspects of life, the jerk in life as well as your smooth mover. Any time you can include the opposite experience, you are 90 percent there. Bodies need opposition to dance. Muscles contract and relax in opposition to one another. This is how we stand, move, and live. Opposing dynamics create the dance. The more we can include the opposites and enjoy all of our movements, the more flow and peace we will have in ourselves.

PLAY: DANCE FAST, SLOW, JERKY, SMOOTH: "KYRIE," *LIKE BREATHING*, #8

Move your whole body. *Kyrie* is a pre-Christian Greek word meaning "Lord, have mercy." The beautiful drone of the harmonium suggests moving slow and smooth. But even when the music around us seems to say one thing, the dance of our lives goes deeper. Include the possibility of fast, quick energy for dynamic contrast. Embrace the chance to play and pray your dance of life as fast, slow, still, jerky, and smooth. If the music or the length of this dance leaves you dis-satisfied, do what you need. Keep going or find the right music for you.

––—––

Give yourself a hand! Believe it or not, you are a solo dancer! Anyone who can move with full range of motion, and start and stop a dance, becomes a solo dancer. We are demystifying the dance. Dance done by the folks is folk dance. You don't have to be an expert to have your birthright.

When your body feels the freedom of having all of who you are, light often pours in. As you play with thrusting, pushy movements, as well as with gentle, tender ones, piety flies out the window. Energy and creativity increase. The tendency to take everything so seriously decreases. Dancing with our whole selves, we come up with more varied, interesting approaches to life.

––—––

"IF I HAD STEPPED ON A SCALE IT MIGHT HAVE SAID,
'TOO HEAVY TO MOVE.'"

JOHANNAS ASMUSSEN JORDON

a college professor in Minnesota who struggled with weight and
health, took a dance class in seminary that changed her life.

FAT. That was the word to describe me. I thought it sounded
better than "morbidly obese," a term used by the medical profession, or "pleasantly plump," used by magazines and friends.
I was well aware of my fat, 44-year-old body as I walked across
that "mile wide" street in Berkeley in September of 1987. To
make matters worse, I was wearing a bright yellow sweat suit.
I was on my way to a dance class.

I had left a successful teaching career at a state university in
the upper Midwest to follow the call to ordination in the Episcopal Church. Things were not going smoothly in the ordination process and school was difficult after more than 20 years
of teaching teachers. I could see every error but my own. Everything in life was hard. I felt as if my body was made of cement and a smile might crack my face. My heart was stone and
my spirit was lead. If I had stepped on a scale it might have said,
"Too heavy to move." I felt too heavy for even God to lift.

I headed for a room at the Pacific School of Religion ironically called Mudd 100. "Oh great, stuck in the mud! Appropriate place for the likes of me," I thought.

It is wonderful how right I was. Not only was it an appropriate place for the likes of me, it was the perfect place for the

likes of me. "Come unto me all ye who are troubled and heavy laden and I will refresh you."

As I entered the room, feeling terrible, a handsome man looked up and said warmly, "Here comes the sun." Suddenly my huge body and yellow suit didn't seem so terrible.

God's invitation was echoing in my body that day, and even though I didn't know I had heard it, I responded. I believe that everyone in that room was responding to a call. We were there for ourselves and for each other. First, the heaviness in my spirit lifted. Then one evening we danced Christ. I can say I found Christ in a dance class. In fact, in that class called Theokinetics, I encountered all of the Christian Trinity. The night we danced the Holy Spirit was steamy and sensual. It was wonderful to rediscover God in all God's forms.

I remember moving around the room one day, and Cynthia, the teacher, said, "Fly, Jo, fly!" and I did. In the company of people who were honest and affirming, I found that I could fly in so many ways. I found my beauty. It isn't rhetoric to say that each person is beautiful in her or his own way. We each are made in the image of God and I think we forget that. God is beautiful and so are we. But it's like Thomas Merton said, "There is no way of telling people that they are all walking around shining like the sun."

The heaviness of sadness lifted and a smile *did* crack my face. And it let the love and the sunshine burst through. Then the fat itself began to melt away. The beautiful little Danish girl I had always been was able to come out. I still have times of heaviness, but, with tools and love, I more often dance through life as light as starlight.

8

SWING, THRUST, SHAPE, HANG

What are you trying not to be? I was forever trying to hold myself in. I felt too big and too weird most of the time. I judged my energetic bursts of joy, anger, and opinion. I was self-conscious about my high level of activity. I abhorred violent behaviour and greatly feared my own ability to hurt others. When I realized that thrusting was an intrinsic part of my unique nature and not a personality defect, I was relieved. The more I let my energy move out from my centre in strong, joyous beams, the more I felt inner peace and clarity in my body. No wonder I had to dance. Thrusting, powerful, quirky moves that open into smooth sweeps bring me grace.

Freedom lives in full colour. Human freedom is a deeply physical thing. Your movement is your freedom – freedom to be personal, freedom to be the personality that you are. We are not each the same as movers. We all move in different ways.

One of the most helpful tools I have found for easily understanding the significant diversity of movement-personality styles is the work of Elizabeth Wetzig, based on the research of kinesiologists Dr. Valerie Hunt and Dr. Judith Rathbone. These women uncovered what I call the primary colours of movement – the red, blue, and yellow of kinesthetic life. The four primal movement patterns are swing, thrust, shape, and hang.

Each of us has either a swing, thrust, shape, or hang home base. In it we feel most ourselves and most relaxed. But our movement choices don't stop with the movements that are most at home for us. We naturally move into the other ways by choice and necessity. For instance, I am often actively moving and doing things, thrusting forward with creative intent. Then, I organize or shape my space, my ideas, and my plans, by holding still as I think things through. But the best part of a day is always when I get to move, to improvise, to play, and to create things or hang out with friends and family. My home base is thrusting. From there I shape, swing, and finally, hang out.

Most of us have been taught to move like others or to move in opposition to our own energy and enthusiasm. When you are at home in the way you move and build from there, grace wells up like a fountain, and life becomes a brilliant tapestry, a symphony of movements.

Are you a swinger? A thruster? A hanger? Or a shaper? Play with the movements and notice what brings the most energy, relief, and sense of well-being over time.

SWING

Swinging involves moving side to side, through centre or around it. You swing when you rock, sway, bounce, jump up and down, spin, or swing someone. Swing moves us from side to side, and back and forth. It lets momentum and gravity do a lot of the work. Swinging motions comfort, soothe, create relationships, help us play, engage our hips, bellies, sexuality, and our love of life. Children need to swing on swings, twirl, have parties, and play with numerous friends. All humans need sexual swinging energy to run and move and connect.

Mood swing, swing low, swing on by, get in the swing of things, it don't mean a thing if it ain't got that swing, swingers, swing set. All these words conjure up the swinger in us. Does this sound familiar? Is it something you long for? Or is it something you judge and avoid? Formalized swinging is found in jazz, gospel, hula, trapeze, belly dance, square dance, golf, tennis, and baseball.

PRACTICE: SWINGING

Rock yourself. Notice what that creates for you. What happens when you swing or sway bigger? Use your arms. Let your breath be a part of the swinging.

Swing a partner. Often, when people do this, memories from childhood are rekindled. Of what activities or life experiences does swinging, twirling, swaying, or bouncing remind you?

THRUST

Thrusting involves energy inside that needs to move out. You thrust when you jab, point, release, fire off, belt out, push, pull, and exert. Thrusting focuses and directs energy outward. It catalyzes and makes things happen, intensifies, articulates, enjoys muscling through, and creating more energy through expending it. A two-year-old thrusts out when they holler, "No! Mine!" Many of us thrust through the day getting to work, doing work, and getting errands done.

Just do it, pull through, put it out there, start-up energy, in your face, get up and go. Sound familiar? Do you need more thrust? Or is it something you judge and avoid? Thrusting can make waves, get you fired up or conjure up anger. Flamenco, River Dance, running, African dance, karate and martial arts, are thrust dances.

PRACTICE: THRUSTING

With one arm or with your whole body, repeatedly shoot out some joy energy. Throw imaginary paint on the wall. Try a little fake flamenco. Do five seconds of all-out fake karate using your voice. What do you notice?

SHAPE

Shaping involves gathering and containing energy at our centre. Shapers sense boundaries, dimensions of things, and differentiate between one thing and another. You shape when you sit still, hold a position, contain yourself, place things in order, and are aware of being in your place and being centred. Shapers form, compose, balance, sort, posture, and proceed one step at a time. Shapers recognize each spatial body and its relationship to other bodies.

Shape up or ship out, know the shape of things to come, ship shape, shapely, out of shape. Shaping things, people, and ideas is a great strength of the Western world. Are you at home in this, or over-shaped? Do you need more order to things? Ballet, sitting meditation, *feng shui*, and yoga are shape bodyspirit practices. Learning to read and do arithmetic, learning rules, and how to stay in your own seat are shape-oriented learning.

PRACTICE: SHAPING

With one arm, make a shape. Breathe as you move your arm from shape to shape. Enjoy the sculptural quality and the stillness as you arrive in each shape. What do you notice?

——

HANG

Instead of sensing a specific direction of energy, hanging is more like being at one with flow and the energy field. When a direction does occur, it happens more by gravity or accident. The feeling of weight and fall, of flying and flowing, are rich with "hanging." Least appreciated in Western environments that teach ordering (shape) and production (thrusting), hangers would just as soon lie in the grass, dream, and feel their oneness with creation. Being one with the field of energy, hangers are acutely aware of mystery, sensing connection between seemingly disparate realities. While not always able to articulate ideas, ideas seem to arise out of the blue and entrepreneurial possibilities abound. Hangers flow, follow, meander, fall into things, loll, float, improvise, move with gravity, commune, offer gifts of presence, and enjoy physical contact. Hang is a way of being that accepts the body on its own terms. Think of a baby hanging out in new awareness, or a teenager who would rather hang out and talk with friends than anything else.

Hang on, hang up, hang over, hang in there, hang out, hang ten, hang dog. How are you with "hanging out?" Do you have difficulty with formal steps? Do you need more "down time," less initiating and more going with the flow? Do you judge yourself for not taking more leadership, more initiative? Ways to hang are found in Tai Chi, snorkeling, contact improvisation, slow grounded tribal dances, raves, lolling on the floor, day-dreaming, or staying in bed.

PRACTICE: HANGING

Let one arm float or fly like a kite. Let go of what it looks like and feel the drift, weight, dance, and flow. Or stand and let your head tilt all the way back. Imagine that you are standing in a redwood grove looking up towards the sky. Relax and let your weight drift around on the balls of your feet. From here it is fun to pretend like you're drunk for a minute. Just let your weight fall wherever it wants to. What do you notice?

Hang, shape, thrust, and swing are the four primary colours of a moving life. They are the coordination that happens between your muscle tension patterns and your mind. You use all of them to walk. Swing your legs to move. Thrust to go forward. Holding your shape keeps you erect. Hang glues it all together and keeps you from being stiff. You have it all. And you can have even more of what creates grace for you. I've seen people heal huge splits in their self-identity and release enormous amounts of energy by coming home fully to their unique moving body.

PLAY: DANCING FOR HOME: "REFLECTION,"
***LIKE BREATHING*, #9**

Remember, don't take this too seriously. Start with one arm or your whole body; play with swinging, thrusting, shaping and hanging. Let yourself move and go where you are drawn.

JOURNAL: NOTICING MY PATTERNS

Playing with these variations, what gives you energy and what tends to use it up? Are there any patterns that you resist or that confuse you? What does your body want more of?

———•———

You are already a far more articulate, unique mover than you may realize. Every move you make is somehow justified, aligned with who you are. Your movement is not random, but occurs according to how you are biologically, neurologically, psychologically, and culturally formed. Movement and personality are one. If you diminish your movement, you distort both your own physical freedom and the greater group body. Not to move in a certain way is like saying, "I will have no green in my life!" Take away something from yourself and you take it away from the whole. Refusing any of the diverse colours of movement, forcing one pattern or style and inhibiting another brings us physical and emotional difficulty in the long run. Too much over-thrusting and over-shaping makes me feel intense, tight, and full. I need the swingy, fun, spiralling sides of myself to maintain my sense of humour and ease. Liberation does not eliminate any aspect of life, but begs for all things to dance in their own unique, healthy, balance.

———•———

"FROM THE MOMENT THAT I WAS BORN, I WAS BIG."

ARTHUR TURBYFILL

a large man with an even larger heart, became a disciple of grace, imagination, voice, and spirit.

It may be true that things grow bigger in the mountains, for I weighed nine pounds, 14 ounces at birth. From the moment that I was born, I was big. My parents quickly changed their plans. They would continue, as they had planned, to name me after my father, but abandoned the plan to call me "Little Art."

Being big of body and having a tendency to be overweight all my life soon meant that clothes were harder for me to find. I needed cars with more headroom. Most people asked what position I played on the high school football team and I found it awkward to tell them that I did not play on the team. Instead, I told them that I played in the marching band. Music, theatre, poetry: these had all been my preferred subjects in school. Of course I danced! I had danced in shows and revues. But I never, ever, would have told anyone that I was a dancer.

I had been seduced by the picture of what a dancer should be. I had an image that a dancer was a small, slight, slender, wisp of a person. This person, usually female, would be very lithe and limber, and look almost anorexic. Her muscles would be toned and she would have years upon years of classical training in dance on which to base her performances. Everything that I saw in my mind as being representative of a dancer was incongruous with how I saw myself.

It is no small thing to realize that you have been imprisoned by the images and pictures that you have about what anything should look like, and by the assumption that such would be the only way things or people could look. So it was with me.

It was very clever of Tom Henderson and Ginny Going, my first InterPlay teachers, to not use the word dance or dancer when they introduced me to dancing. Instead, they used the word movement. I certainly could move, and could even move fairly well and gracefully, if given the opportunity. I began to explore all the ways that my body could move through space. I had fun with swinging and thrusting, shaping and hanging, and even walking, stopping, and running. I learned to create varieties of movement with all parts of my body, working with various levels of height and speed.

Then the realization began to sink in. It was probably when everyone in the group was asked to raise their right hand and solemnly swear, "I am a solo dancer," that it dawned on me that I am a dancer indeed. I realized that in order to dance I didn't have to be a diminutive person with a great amount of training (although those people are dancers, too!). Rather, I learned that dancing is about having a body, being in your body, and celebrating that you have a body that can do all these things. It is not a matter of size or shape or training. It is more a matter of being able to have for myself the joy of moving about in as many and varied ways as my heart and soul guide me. It is about letting my body express itself, and the spirit that dwells within it, for my own delight. It no longer matters what other people think.

That's when it happens. Those in our community of play, speak about exploding the pictures. It's as if the tiny frames and frozen images that we have used to evaluate and perhaps devalue the world around us can no longer contain the beautiful reality of what it means to be a human being endowed with a human body. Somehow, in the breaking free, in the celebration we have as we jump and spin, stretch and push, and have fun in our bodies, no matter what size, no matter what shape, no matter what age, those around us begin to have fun, too. Now I can say with great delight that I am a dancer.

Perhaps the most joyful thing is being able, perhaps for the first time, to feel myself in a state of grace while moving my body. One of the things that comes with our pictures of "big" bodies is the idea that they are not graceful. But when I am dancing, when I let go and feel the movement that comes from inside myself, I do feel graceful. In a world that always had trouble accepting that my big body could move with grace, I now feel down in the very centre of my being that I am graceful. And not only graceful, I feel beautiful. In a world that is quick to show us ways in which we are not beautiful, and then offer us a myriad of methods to make ourselves beautiful, it is a glorious gift.

With the treasure of these experiences in my own body, I have taken it as a calling to share with other big-bodied people the joy that they, too, can experience through the dance. Bodies of all shapes and sizes and abilities can move and dance and have grace and be beautiful. There is such an abundance of space in the world, and such a wonderful variety of bodies, that to deny our birthright to dance seems such an awful deprivation not only for us, but also for the universe.

MOVE : WHAT THE BODY WANTS

9

A FULL BODY YES

Creativity is inherent to bodies. We are constitutionally unable to avoid being creative. We make the bed, make dinner, make love, make messes, make art. We make choices. Our creative spirit is always playing it up, playing things down, playing it out, and playing for keeps. Play is our whole-bodied, freely given engagement in making things.

Somehow we have made work the basis of reality and play its antidote. Yet ever since the Garden of Eden, play has been the essence of relationship to God. George Fowler, in *Dance of a Fallen Monk: A Journey to Spiritual Enlightenment*, writes,

We wouldn't go onto the dance floor and ask the dancers where they're headed with all their footsteps. We'd be equally foolish to ask them to demonstrate material gain for what they are doing. At best, they'd look surprised and say we'd missed the point. The dance of God is just like that – no purpose but the joy.

Think of it. In play we entrust ourselves so deeply to the moment that we forget about ourselves and enter into union with our playmates. Having chosen the moment, we forget that we have chosen it. It just happens.

I see play as more basic than work. We have to be told to get back to work, but no one has to tell us to get back to play. Play is where we belong. It's the creative current beneath all life. Life plays. Life plays us.

Play is not the opposite of work. It is the home of our best work. It is easier to play hard than to hardly play. Play can underlie the most challenging task. Those who feel they are playing find that work is meaningful and full of creative intent and power. However, when we "work" at life, grace, meaning, and ease get lost.

If you want more grace, more of a sense of playfulness, you have to make choices according to what you know (your body knowledge). Your body wisdom takes your physical experience seriously in the most playful way. Wisdom is choosing to do what is good for you, for others, and for all of creation. It is surprising what a creative challenge it is to be wise and to follow grace. Most of the world is at work solving problems. And yet each time I choose grace I am rewarded to see how it affects both me and others. Grace is physical. We can feel it. Follow the logic of grace and you and your life will surge. It's as simple as that. You can make grace.

JOURNAL: COLLECT THE HEALTHY BODY DATA

Notice your sensations of ease in this moment, the body data, the bits and pieces of physical information you experience right now. Ease is always present. Where do you find sensations of relaxation, openness, or energy within yourself right now? Also notice the thoughts and sensations of difficulty. They are part of your health, too. What are they asking for?

Experience is complex, multi-textured, and layered. Many things go on at the same time. We can be happy about work and sad about our marriage. We can notice the weather, steer the car, feel overstimulated from traffic, and sing a sad love song with the radio, all at once. Having so much data is not a problem for the body. Our body, like the universe, holds many realities at once. In fact, this is the nature of life. Space and time are big and open. The present moment isn't one second, but a generous playing field. Try to isolate, eliminate, or narrow our experience of life into small pieces, and our bodies rebel. When we eliminate anger, our body revolts. You get hostile, instead of just angry in the moment. Attempt to cast out imbalances, and you will immediately feel precarious. When you use energy to ward off experiences, you only fatigue and become more susceptible to the things you resist.

This is why with easy focus, whole-body creativity helps us to have ourselves in a way that analyzing and controlling our experiences doesn't. Even if we can't put what we have into words, we can be full, complex, ever-changing, and aware. If you are a person whose life is so full that it defies articulation, a life bigger than words, this wordless acceptance is grace enough. From there, the best way to express all the complexity is often to dance or sing. As Pamela Brown says, "Dance can give the inarticulate a voice."

Choosing to say yes to ourselves is a leap. Something in us knows that there will be disorientation. The jump to get back to the playground often brings initial anxiety.

Peter Maher, an Australian priest, wrote about his uncertain entry into creativity and body wisdom when he left church duties in 1996.

Leaving the parish, I needed space to breathe and to think with people I felt could help. The cost was uncertainty and confusion. But the body wisdom is, that cost can be life-giving. Body awareness taught me to breathe. When confronted by fear, the body tightens up, the face stiffens, and the lungs seem to have no air. It is as if we stop breathing. Movement teaches how to read the messages of the body, how to breathe and to find space for rethinking. Without body aware-ness, the brain is sometimes paralyzed, making us incapable of find-ing ways to live creatively through the fear. The body itself is opening up to new possibilities. In practicing, I found I was less paralyzed by fear and more able to imagine different possibilities.

Eventually, Peter broke through his insecurities and found a less inhibited self. He wrote this invitation.

> Come play with me awhile,
> Inhale, exhale, eeeeeh, ahhhhhh,
> Again and again in joy and fun
> the body opening and closing...
> Taken by the arm, the thigh, the big toe,
> centring in the earth mother
> shake it out, find the place for you,
> take a partner, be a witness
> discover primeval voice
> touch true communion.
> Allured, called to come – we are afraid
> and thereby surely fed.

Joy comes with stepping into your own creative current. Choose grace and your choices often get clearer. You listen to yourself more. You are led in completely new directions in relationship, vocation, and creative endeavors. You no longer fit neatly into tight spaces. You stick out and you could care less. Sometimes you just don't want to do anything at all for a while.

JOURNAL: CLAIM WHAT YOU ENJOY

Write down things, activities, people, and places that repeatedly bring joy, peace, or aliveness to your body. These are part of your creative life force. Noticing the repeating patterns of enjoyment in things that energize and bring you life, claim what you enjoy. This is your own body of knowledge. If you know what you enjoy, are you getting enough of them?

———

Grace-making can appear sacrificial if you choose to act for the good of the community over yourself. If it directly benefits your deepest creative desires, however, it doesn't feel sacrificial because it is you who desire it. So be sacrificial if you want. Or be totally self-fulfilling! Fill yourself with grace and others will receive the benefits directly from your body to theirs.

PRACTICE: YES! TO BODY WISDOM

Create a YES for grace today – your own or someone else's. Practice saying "Yes" to what comes your way, especially the good things.

———

"THE EAGLE HAS LIFTED AND I'M ON BOARD."

JUNE GOUDEY

after a lifelong journey with death, already knew that imagination was a key to her life. When she discovered the creativity in her body wisdom, there was no turning back.

Healing and teaching have been central to my being...healing me, healing others; teaching me, teaching others. So how did I get here? There has been struggle enough...to be well, to be accepted, to be honest, to be happy, to be in relationship, to be true, to be a writer, to be a thinker, to be a preacher, to be a poet, to laugh, to play, to trust, to hope, to feel full...of love, of trust, of compassion, of hope, of generosity, of wisdom...to overcome adversity, evil, depression, sadness, loneliness, abandonment, and most of all, the fear and pain in my body.

Tuberculosis took my father and me from our family.
The sanitarium took my body.
The funeral home where I lived took my playfulness.
The housing projects took my confidence.
Fear took my spirit; memories of pain took my hope.
Sexuality confused me.
Sadness frightened me.
Sarcasm silenced me.
Pain diminished me.
Loneliness defined me.
Times of poverty undermined whatever sense of self remained.
Wounds created wounds, piled on fear, provoked pain.
Mind, heart, and spirit lost their body connections.

AND YET...
Grace kept seeping in, through family ties and friendships,
all because I kept going forward.
One step at a time did the trick; Mom gave me that:
"If at first you don't succeed;
simply do your level best, God with ease will do the rest;
it's always darkest before the dawn..."
I hated her platitudes, but I clung to them.

Scripture weighed in too. Psalm 146: "Be still and know that I
am God..." Isaiah 40: "Have you not known, have you not heard?
God will lift you up on eagles wings...you will run and not be
weary, you will walk and not faint." Grace-makers aplenty kept
throwing me lifelines. "Hang on, tread water, land is near."

Along the way, love held the pain, hope held the fear, and
grace held the loneliness as healing knit my bones. Joy lifted
the weight of life and generosity pushed aside hopelessness, as
spirit pulled, prodded, and surrounded me with love, love, and
love – until I couldn't stop the loving from breaking forth, again
and again, theirs or mine.

Eventually, love pushed the fear to the edges of my life.
Grace accepted me, hope surprised me, faith assured me, and
life affirmed me.

Psychotherapists held me back from the abyss... Zoloft restored my equilibrium, EMDR [Eye Movement Desensitization
and Reprocessing] awakened body connections strong enough
to banish the pain. Imagination sustained me with laughter,
poetry warmed my soul, and nature nurtured my long-suffer-
ing "awe" muscles. Love overwhelmed me but never consumed
me. Adversity tried its best and won at times, but the seeds of
hope planted by love and watered by tears kept me soft and
receptive and open.

And then one day – when readiness had helped me WAKE

UP! – InterPlay bounced into my life…and my body has never been the same. Thanks be to God!

Aliveness, compassion, and grace became my playmates, and hawks once again (that's another story…) beckoned me with resurrection!

Now it's my turn to throw lifelines. YES! I've been practicing all my life for this – now it's time to widen the waters of possibility and throw open the gates of heaven. It's time to let the lessons of my life and the promises of God take me to new heights. The eagle has lifted and I'm on board.

LEAPING SPEED BUMPS

GETTING PAST OUR WORST FEARS OF BEING SEEN AND KNOWN

10

WAS BLIND, BUT NOW I SEE

S usan Cubel says, "Life is not measured by how many breaths we take, but by the moments that take our breath away." If anything takes my breath away, it is a person in their innocence. Original innocence is the soulful, openhearted, imaginative freedom to be one's self in body. This is a dream place. To recapture this state as adults is a great spiritual quest. It requires not only courage, but something more: the willingness to be seen. Don't we long for the eyes of love to hold us with admiration and respect? What stops us from letting that happen? What makes it possible?

In Junior High, suffering from a romantic, Disneyesque hormonal surge, I danced the house broom like a lover all around the downstairs den of our home. My mom, looking down the stairs at me, asked, "What are you doing?" My fantasy shattered. I was mortified and burst into tears. I had been seen! There's nothing worse than being caught in an act of soulful absorption when you are unprepared.

Ironically, we are witnessed all the time anyway. Like a child hiding behind a sapling, we stick out all over. We easily see one another's spirit. Spirit is not invisible. It is informed in everything. Our spirit is right here in our body. Seen. Becoming willing to be seen brings more peace and grace.

PRACTICE: SEE SPIRIT

Instead of pretending that spirit is invisible, look around you with the idea that spirit is visible in everything. If there is no split between body and spirit, spirit is visible. This does not take away from the mysterious source or nature of spirit. What changes if we acknowledge that human spirit and holy spirit are in view?

If we feel safe enough, I believe most people want to be seen and known. Probably feeling unseen himself, Vincent Van Gogh wrote in a letter, "One may have a blazing hearth in one's soul and yet no one ever comes to sit by it. Passersby see only a wisp of smoke rising from the chimney and continue on their way."

Doesn't some part of us crave the idea of catching ourselves wholly beautiful in the eyes of a beholder? Reserving this privilege for a sole lover, we compose a million love songs that tell us this is what we want. "See Me! Love Me!" Yet this is very vulnerable. After the fifth grade, letting ourselves be seen gets harder and harder as we become aware that others judge us. And if we have been poorly or abusively witnessed, we withdraw, remain private, and feel anxious about being seen. Letting ourselves be seen works best if we can be aware of this as a deep inner need, and then choose it for ourselves. For the secret antidote to much of our distress is an affirming, nonintrusive witness of another. It is the way home.

By practicing the things we fear in small, incremental steps, it is possible to transform walls of fear into more manageable speed bumps. You know how it is to approach a speed bump with your grocery cart. If you slow way down, it takes a lot of effort to push the cart over. Experience teaches that if you push your cart over the bump a little more quickly, the process is not so disruptive. Leaping the speed bumps of our fear is like that. But first we need to gain the confidence that the things we fear can be made manageable, if not liberated.

JOURNAL: LEAPING SPEED BUMPS

Remember something you once feared that you now do well. Has your success in dealing with this experience tempered your memory of the fear? Looking back, what helped you to become less fearful? Could you imagine approaching a new challenge as more of a speed bump than a wall? Could you practice an easy shrug and say, "I can do that," instead of "Oh...No!" After reflecting on these questions, shake all this fear stuff out of your body, and take a deep breath.

In addition to leaping my own speed bumps and taking the dance of life one step at a time, three practices have made a huge difference in my becoming more open to witnessing others and being witnessed. They are: giving space to each person, easy focus, and savouring and affirming the good in one another.

I believe bodies are designed to be pure in spirit, not cluttered with the energetic baggage of others. Those who hang on us, push us around, over-worry about us, wear us out, drain us even without touching us, carelessly lay judgment on us, invade us, mess with our minds, over-attend to us, or won't let us go, affect our bodies in real physical ways. Perceiving each other's physical boundaries shows respect for the solitude of each being.

In the Bible, Moses ascends Mount Zion alone and is met by God. His head on the ground, shoes off and feet naked, he knows and is intimately known. This is the ultimate form of grace. As Psalm 13 says, "God, you have searched me and known me." On the other hand, head down, butt in the air, is as close as Moses gets to laying eyes on God's private parts. Even then it aged him years. After that, God asked Moses to come back again bringing one other person. All the other priests were to remain at the foot of the mountain lest they die.

I believe each person's bodyspirit is like the holy mountain that Moses climbed, the place where soul meets God. Like the wilderness, the soul of each person is meant to be great, wild, pure, and unpeopled by the spirits and opinions of others. Our solitude, the state of holy selfhood, is a criterion for our health. Trespassing upon another person's life without permission – through rape, gossip, abuse, incest of any kind, curse, or hate – is extreme violation with disastrous bodyspirit consequences for both parties.

How can we play in community without being invasive? Staying in your own body is the most healing thing you can do for another. A room full of people flooding us with physical concern is overwhelming. But a people gently and easily holding you in their own ease is grace-making. Ease, or what some call a "non-anxious presence," propels natural healing.

———

PRACTICE AND JOURNAL: THE BOUNDARIES OF YOUR SPACE
With a partner, stand ten feet apart from one another. As one partner stands still, the other slowly approaches. When standing still, do you notice sensations as your partner approaches your space? There may be several thresholds. What is it like to have you physical bounda-

ries crossed? Pleasant? Too much? Have the other person stand still and notice as you walk up to them. Explore this with different partners. It is different from person to person and time to time.

———

The old English word "witness" comes from the root "to know." Both the witness and the one witnessed can know and be known. While this kind of intimacy is usually reserved for a lover, it does not have to be so rare. It is something you and I can have more regularly. Having ourselves and the world around us is an experience of at-one-ment. In it, we are physically complete, breathing it all in and out, enjoying the dance.

One day, feeling familiar sensations of intensity, I walked to the end of the Berkeley pier in frustration and asked God for a way to deal with the drain of energy that I felt constantly pouring out of me. I was tired and needed help. I looked across the bay toward the Golden Gate Bridge and realized that I needed to let the beautiful view feed me, but didn't know how to get the spoon to my mouth. My focussing was like a galloping team of horses. I had to physically take hold of the reins and say, "Whoa!" Pulling back into my body, I opened my eyes wider and heard the words, "Take. Eat." Slowly, I began to gather the beauty into myself. "Take. Eat." I pulled the beauty into my eyes, into my senses. Could it be that seeing, hearing, smelling, tasting, touching, and being moved were not things I needed to defend or "watch out for"? Could they really be a way for nourishment to enter me?

Similarly, my hearing had shut down to moderate the endless mrrrrrrr of city sound. When I relaxed my jaws and ear areas, I opened to symphonies of everyday sounds. Instead of resisting sounds, for a moment I heard their music. I realized that instead of not hearing well, I am very sensitive to sound. Opening and closing my ears is a choice now.

Softening the senses is a contemplative act. It's like communion. Actively choosing to receive sight, sound, and kinesthetic experience, we can have and savour experience. We call this "having." In InterPlay, we think it is enough to "have" experience. The physical sensations of having what we have make us who we are in the moment.

An easy focus relaxes our visual, analytical scanners. Going easy on the eyes allow us to open up our larger field of perception and to feel our whole body. You don't have to just look out for people and things. It is physically possible to enjoy taking in the world around us.

***

PRACTICE: WITNESSING THE GOOD

Take a deep breath. Let it out with a sigh. Massage your forehead, and jaw. Engage your easy focus. Witness your surroundings. What are you most attracted to? Can you let it in?

***

I can almost guarantee you that when you have learned to soften your focus, your own judgmental view of others will ease up. When you ease up on how you see others, it will be more possible to believe that others could see you in a softer way as well. Scrutiny is what the body doesn't want. And self-scrutiny is the absolute worst. It feels like a huge eyeball hanging out in front of us, checking out our every move. The eyeball appears to be ours. Some call this eye the inner judge or critic. Whatever you call it, it definitely keeps its eye on you. If it gets stuck looking back at you for too long, you will want to disappear.

I encountered this eye while struggling with public speaking. Preaching to a small congregation each Sunday I would stand before them and take a deep breath only to feel my throat tighten, my chest shrink, and my words go flat. I did everything I knew to counteract this experience. Two things finally helped.

First, I realized I was literally looking down on myself. In my imagination, I saw the eyeball hanging outside of my head, so I took hold of the scrutinizing eye with both hands, stuck it back inside my head, turned it around and focussed out. Sure enough, I felt better. I had previously made a deal with myself not to bore myself or anyone else with my words. This decision backfired because it was like super gluing the scrutinizing judgmental eye in place. That eye didn't prevent me from being boring, it was preventing me from ever speaking at all because, of course, I found all words boring.

Additional relief from self-scrutiny came the night I became willing to be boring. When I realized I was terrified of boring people, I decided I might as well be a bore. It couldn't be any worse than the fear that had a stranglehold on me and my imagination. When I showed up to teach my next class, I happily began it by saying, "I have an announcement. I am happy to tell you I am willing to bore you today." Laughter erupted from all corners. And typical to my experience of playing with these things publicly, I became more entertaining and less boring as the critical view of myself really relaxed.

Meanwhile, you don't need to give up your protection or discrimination to witness or be witnessed. In fact, your bodyspirit is quite selective about how much input it can handle. In modern urban life, our instinctive physical tendency is to withdraw or defend by pushing our way through the day (fight or flight). I cross my forearms over my solar plexus to regulate my level of connection, which, frankly, is often too much. I honour my need for separation and quiet, and appreciate encouragement to physically open up to the goodness that is everywhere.

It is very natural to focus on problems and create protections. In stressful environments, it is a given. In our very busy world, looking for the good must be a daily practice if you are to have grace.

PRACTICE AND JOURNAL: WITNESSING IS FOR YOU

Shake out your body. Shake out the critical, hard, cynical points of view. With your easy focus, notice specifically what comes to you as good. It may be something moving, amusing, appetizing, or pleasant in some way. Whatever you take in is there for you. Can you have it? Feel it. For some reason, you have noticed and received a particular experience. It may be random or it may be a gift of the universe. It is yours alone to unwrap and enjoy. When you witness a person, look for this same kind of gift to come your way through something they say, do, or are.

The words of the hymn "Amazing Grace" describe my experience perfectly: "was blind, but now I see." Looking for the good feeds me. Looking for the good in others feeds the garden. Witnessing with eyes that seek the good is a major form of prayer. Saint Francis said, "The result of prayer is life. Prayer irrigates earth and heart." Our bodyspirits like to look out at the world, to make things, and to play. Once you've got your eyes in your head, your senses engaged and wanting to be in the world, it is much easier to relax, to be seen, and to respond to life. In fact, you can savour it. This is a spiritual practice in InterPlay. First we learn to witness the good, and then we savour it.

PRACTICE AND JOURNAL: SAVOURING

At a park, café, on a walk, or sitting at home, release yourself from obligations to help or analyze anyone for a moment. Open your easy focus to the receiving mode. Tune into sensory goodness. Breathe with it. Savour it. And then let it go.

Affirmation is a recognition and communication of the actual good we witness. When a person creates enjoyment for you in a specific way and you tell them, then you move good into the light. You create grace. Affirmation that is specific, personal, and truthful creates a triple supply of grace in the world. And it is so simple to do that it is grievous how little affirmation people receive when it can make such a huge difference.

After a back-to-school night, a friend wrote a simple thank-you to three of her daughter's teachers, for taking the time to share their hopes and plans for the school year. The next day she got phone calls from all three of them. They called to thank her back. Never in their teaching careers had anyone thanked them for their work on back-to-school night. Their goodness had been seen. Grace had its day.

Affirmation is as much a physical practice as anything else. It is something that one does. In order for it to be meaningful, it must honestly connect with one's own experience of feeling the goodness of something that one has received. When I first started affirming people as a practice, it felt bold and weird. I would feel my connection to something that struck me as good and then tell the person. They always seemed surprised. But no one ever backed away or rebuked me. Instead they seemed pleased. It was such a simple thing to do. All I had to do was open my mouth. Why was it so hard? Practice. Anything you do not practice is not in your experience.

PRACTICE: THE POWER OF AFFIRMING

When you notice someone that moves you today, tell them. All you have to do is say thank you. Keep it brief. Savour this grace with them if they can receive it, and then let it go. It doesn't help the body to hoard the good. Make room for more.

Affirmation means to "make firm." Witnessing with affirmation strengthens us and makes the ground upon which we all walk more solid. Though we may feel no great need to be witnessed, there is something others may need to witness in us to find hope and faith. We each have something that is uniquely needed in the world.

A woman I shall call Bee came regularly to my workshops with her rigid body and exaggerated expressions. Her speech was full of breaks and starts and other people often reacted to her first with curiosity then with awkward avoidance. I believe their bodies picked up her tightness. They tried to like her and ignore their feelings, but when they didn't know what else to do, they distanced themselves from her. Eventually, Bee told me she had epilepsy. It was a relief to me to learn the source of her challenge and it made me more curious about her life and her experience. I encouraged her to share her experience of epilepsy with the group. This was a huge step. All her life she had tried to be normal, to downplay her illness. What would happen when people witnessed her in this truth? With my support, she spoke to our class. Watching them as they listened and came to understand her dilemma, I saw the class members visibly relax. They let go of worrying about her so much. We all began to honour the incredible expertise she had in dealing with her illness, and starting including her in lighter, more playful ways. Opportunities to be matter-of-fact about this personal challenge helped our community release from over-focussing on it.

One day I saw the miraculous. Bee wanted me to witness her as she sat in a chair and danced with her hands. Released from needing to stabilize her balance, her energy seemed to become huge, bright, and almost angelic. Dancing helped her come closer to God and was an antidote to her crazy, electromagnetic jumpiness. Her face softened in radiance. She was a sight to behold. But what was even better is that I was able to have and receive the grace of her incredible dance directly into my body. Her transfiguration became mine. It surprised me as only the Spirit can do.

Based on the sweet acceptance given to Bee in our community of play, she desperately wanted her Catholic church to dance with her. It was now clear to me that she knew something exceptional about God and grace. She considered herself a liturgical dancer and wanted to share the power of this with her own people. When the parish exhibited the same reluctance that Bee's classmates had initially felt, I encouraged her to tell the parish leadership about her epilepsy. Although she did so, they continued to discourage her from leading dance or from dancing themselves. I believe they simply did not know how to receive her good news. With tremendous sorrow, Bee left to find a church that could witness and celebrate her as a dancer. I often wonder how many amazing grace's we miss because we don't know how to see them.

At some point, with practice, being seen becomes a pleasure, even a need for health. It is as simple and miraculous as Janie Oakes' poem reveals.

I witness your edges
Notice your knees
I see you transformed
Before your own eyes
Inside out, like a sweater
Your rough seams
Are showing
Hard, soft, hard, soft
You open and close
And open again.

"IT WAS MY FIRST PUBLIC PERFORMANCE
AS A WHEELCHAIR DANCER."

CORNELIA LEE

at age 45, left non-profit work to make her living in dance
in spite of polio and extreme muscle loss in her left leg.

In the morning, I put on a black leotard and tights, pull a T-shirt over my head, and drive to a dance studio in the massive brick building of the Cleveland Masonic Temple. I take a two-hour modern technique class with professional dancers, then break for lunch before going back into the studio for company rehearsal. In the late afternoon, as I drive past the glass and pink marble buildings of the Cleveland Clinic on my way back to my apartment, I think about how I came to be here, at age 40, 600 miles from my home and friends, to dance in a wheelchair with the Dancing Wheels.

There is nothing. Only blackness. Then, two figures leaning over me. My mommy and daddy. Why can't I move? Tears wet my cheeks. I'm only one or two and I don't understand why I can't sit up or move my legs. I tell my legs to kick, but they just lay limp under the sheet. Yesterday I had been running around the house. Now I lay paralyzed by Polio. After an eternity, I can sit up again. Then I can stand, unsteadily. Finally, I learn to walk again, but I can't run anymore. I can't jump.

My return to the dance of life began in 1997, when I could no longer ignore a growing desire to perform. "I want to be a storyteller! My passion is performing and telling stories!" I told my closest friends. Acting on this desire, I took acting and theatre improvisation classes. And then I heard about InterPlay.

I went to one of my first InterPlay gatherings in the spring of 1999 and stayed for a BodySpirit celebration afterwards. It was at an old church in Raleigh that had been converted into a middle school. When the BodySpirit celebration began, I was tired, so at first I just watched. I was uplifted and energized by the lively, improvised stories and songs that people offered, and which drew on the combined energies of us all. When one of the leaders asked if two people would dance while she read a poem, my body jumped up and I found myself facing a lithe blond woman named Judith. I instinctively followed and built upon her movements and the images from the poem. My body seemed to know what to do. At one point I was upside down in a handstand while Judith supported me.

Afterwards, people said to me, "That was a wonderful dance! You looked beautiful. You have danced before, haven't you?" Something magical had happened; the simple movement patterns of the gathering had somehow shaken me loose of self-consciousness, letting what was inside me emerge.

InterPlay quickly became my creative hearth, warming and nurturing mini-creations of self-expression. At first, I focussed on the storytelling forms, never thinking of myself as a dancer. I was a cripple. How could a cripple be a dancer?

Polio had decimated most of the muscles in my left leg from the hip down; the remaining muscle enabled me to walk with a limp. As a child, I loved to move, and I especially loved to dance. For a few years I took ballet lessons. I felt great joy as I danced in a recital, wearing a black sequined leotard and red tutu. We danced a tarantella, and afterwards an adult praised my dancing, saying, "You have very good rhythm." Soon after that, I proudly pulled on pink toe shoes and started pointe class. But the teacher said I couldn't come back to her class, because I couldn't get up on pointe on my left foot. I felt crushed. I put away my ballet slippers and buried my dancing dreams.

I had never heard of wheelchair dancing until I saw a flyer advertising auditions for a play called Wheelchair Dancer in January 1998. I felt my heart speed up as I read the play's description "about a wheelchair dancer who joins a professional dance troupe." I decided on the spot to audition. The lead role was already filled, but I was offered a role as understudy. Although I turned down the role, I saw the play. I was moved to tears when the wheelchair-using actress danced in a beautiful composition with non-disabled dancers.

This inspired me and opened me to the possibility that a wheelchair could actually increase my mobility, rather than limit it. Though I could dance on my feet, I couldn't dance that way for very long. I tired after a few dances at a party. And over the past few years, the time I could remain on my feet dancing without tiring got progressively shorter, due to Post Polio Syndrome. Now I knew of a way to sit down and continue dancing!

However, I didn't own a manual wheelchair. A manual wheelchair carries a stigma of abnormality and severe disability. I was afraid that once I started using one, I would not be able to get up and walk again.

One night I attended a performance of the InterPlay Off the Deep End Ensemble. I loved watching them dance and fantasized about dancing in a wheelchair with them. I did a hand contact dance with an ensemble member during an audience participation exercise, and afterwards the ensemble co-director said I danced beautifully and that he loved watching me.

As I lived more fully in my body, I had more fullness and enjoyment in everyday activities. Bit by bit, InterPlay breathed new life into the buried embers of my dreams. Being witnessed, hearing affirmations of my dancing, and re-experiencing the joy of letting dance move through me without trying, inspired me. My pleasure and confidence in my dancing increased.

In the spring of 2000, I set up two solo performances that combined dancing and storytelling. I wasn't really trying to dance, I was just moving in between bits of storytelling. But people said my movements were so graceful and interesting that they wanted to see more of them. That was it. I had performed as a solo dancer without intending to. And people liked it!

I wanted to do more. That summer, I signed up for two InterPlay retreats in California. Only the need to play and dance for long periods could have motivated me to start shopping for a wheelchair. If I thought I was getting one because I really needed it, which I did, I would have balked. In fact, my doctor had given me a prescription for a wheelchair months earlier.

There wasn't time to find just what I needed before my trip, so I got a loaner wheelchair. When I arrived at the Northern California retreat, I pushed the chair to the side and rarely sat in it during the first session. But I needed to sit down or risk wearing myself out. When I did, other InterPlayers didn't look down upon or talk condescendingly to me, a response I dreaded. In fact, one of the participants asked, "Is that your chair? Cool!" It was cool; it was very lightweight and had removable armrests.

The second or third morning, I began to dance in the chair. Paired with Kylie, an experienced dancer about my size, she and I experimented with different ways of sharing our weight and supporting each other. Then we performed a contact improvisation duet for the rest of the group, "just because it's so interesting," Cynthia said.

I felt awkward because I wasn't sure how to move the wheelchair, and the steel and plastic creation felt foreign. Yet Kylie treated the chair like it was just another part of my body. She leaned on it and on me. She pulled on the chair, tipping it backwards and sideways; I leaned and pulled on her. We rolled across the room together as I lifted her. Afterwards, person after person said to me, "that was so beautiful, those lifts were especially graceful. You are a graceful dancer. You move gracefully."

I was elated. "People appreciate me as a dancer, and they appreciate me as a dancer in a wheelchair! Maybe this wheelchair business isn't so bad," I thought. New possibilities for dance exploded around me.

I began to feel sparks between the chair and myself. I hated my need for the chair, but I loved the gift of new movement it gave me. I sailed across the room during a group solo dance in a way I could not have done on my feet. It reminded me of the synchronized swimming I had done as a child, freed temporarily from the chains of gravity that slowed me on the ground.

Then we paired off to do solo dances for a witness. As I began dancing in the wheelchair, I felt a deep well of energy urgently rising through me, like a kid bursting through the kitchen door into her house wanting to tell mom about her day. I danced the grief of not having enough stamina or strength to dance the way I saw others dance; I danced the sadness of confinement to a chair. I danced a story that could not be told except through movement. I pushed the chair away and danced on my knees, using my whole upper body. Intense joy and passion erupted from deep inside, setting my torso and limbs moving powerfully without any effort on my part. I felt joy of movement, joy of performing, joy of being affirmed and appreciated. Passion was dancing itself through me. There were no other thoughts; there was no inner critic, no split in my being. I was the dance.

Afterwards, I leaned back exhausted and beaming. My witness said, "That was beautiful!"

Then Phil said, "In InterPlay, we honour the contribution of all bodies. At the same time, we recognize that there are some who are clearly called to be dancers or storytellers in the community. And we want to encourage them, because the community is enriched by their gifts." In my gut, I felt he was talking about me. I felt called to be a dancer and performer, and this both scared and thrilled me.

I signed up for an advanced InterPlay performance class led by Ginny Going and Tom Henderson. The class culminated at the end of October 2000 in a performance with Off the Deep End Ensemble. It was my first public performance as a wheelchair dancer. I danced a duet one night and a solo the next. Audience members told me that my gracefulness and the way I lit up as I danced moved them to tears. Tom and Ginny invited me into Off the Deep End Ensemble starting in January. And I started to contact wheelchair dance companies around the country, seeking opportunities for further training.

Dancing Wheels of Cleveland invited me to spend a week in February training with them. I went and at the end of that week they offered me an apprenticeship, with the possibility of joining the company as a paid, full-time wheelchair dancer. I moved to Cleveland to begin my apprenticeship, performing with Dancing Wheels in a major production of new work.

And so it goes...

AFTERWORD

Cornelia Lee is now an independent performing artist and choreographer living and working in Chapel Hill, North Carolina. In November of 2003, she was awarded an Emerging Artist Grant from Durham, Chapel Hill Arts Council.

11

THE POWER OF FEELING

In a psychological test I took, I scored nine out of a possible ten on empathy. I can sometimes sense the emotional experience of other people before they are aware of it themselves. This is a gift. It is also a curse. Easily overwhelmed, I have avoided hospitals and places where people are troubled. I had to learn to protect myself, yet always felt it was difficult to do. I was a kinesthetic sponge. I discovered I was trying to resolve other people's experiences as my own. In turn, I gave too much advice. I was trying to help everybody in order to help myself. Now I am amused at all the therapy I've done. Much of it had to do with things I've felt but that were not mine to fix. Unfortunately, you can't solve anyone else's problems, even if you have felt them in your own body. All you can do is notice the experiences of others that you are feeling and release them.

Suffering moved me and I didn't like it. But if I tried to protect myself, I found myself minimizing things that moved me to joy as well. Taking my kinesthetic sensitivity more seriously,

I began to ask those around me if they were experiencing my symptoms. Once, while driving in a car with a companion, I felt my throat tighten. I asked myself why my throat felt constricted and couldn't think of any reason. Then, I asked my friend if her throat was tight. "Yes," she said. "I'm sad."

Our senses are like baseball catchers. We catch life in the flesh. Scientists have actually discovered little mirror neurons that allow us to directly and immediately replicate the feeling of what we are seeing around us. As players, we are meant to throw these balls of life experience back out again. Moving things out with story, word, song, and activity is how we stay healthy. When you allow experiences to move back out of your body, you make room for new ones. Journalling, dancing, exercising, weaving, praying, crying, even ironing and washing the dishes, help us move the experiences onward. In InterPlay, we call this exformation. It is the opposite of information.

In an age of over information, everyone is aware that we must limit the amount of paper, mail, email, television, and stimulation we receive. Limiting it is not enough. Our bodies are full. We tire and get depressed. There's just too much. We need to move things out. In addition, we need to be aware of the kind of bodies with whom we are relating.

Did you know that you feel the movement of others in your body? At a football game, a performance, watching children play, or seeing a hawk lift off on the wind, we are moved by the movement of others. The movement of another body affects us directly. We feel other's actions in our own muscles. I am so sensitive kinesthetically that when a fork drops in the kitchen I jump. Or when a car veers in front of me, I jerk. My family members laugh at my involuntary convulsions. When my husband and daughter wrestle and poke at each other, I get agitated. At the same time, when I watch dance, I feel like I am dancing. It's wondrous.

JOURNAL: GO WHERE YOU ARE WONDERFULLY MOVED

On a scale of one to ten, ten being high, are you easily moved? Where do you go to be moved in ways you really enjoy? What people do you enjoy being around? Do you notice anything about their movement quality? Are you attracted to quieter bodyspirits or more energetic types? Notice the movement of people, animals, and cars in your environment and how they affect your body. If you could choose what kind of movement you wanted to absorb, who, what, or where would you move toward? What would you move away from?

———•———

We can be brought to the edge of our seats at a movie, moved to tears by someone else's feelings, and absorbed in the meditation as we watch someone weave, stir a pot, or build a fire. Yes, we can even be moved to stillness. In the quiet of a forest I have seen people grow still just by walking into groves of redwood trees. They look as though they might never move again.

How does this work? I first heard my mentor, Judith Rock, explain this kinesthetic sense to her class. Judith would jump up and down in front of the class and ask us what we felt. Even though we sat still and she was jumping, we noticed a slightly jumpy feeling inside ourselves. All of sudden, she would throw herself dangerously off balance. We gasped and then laughed. We were not falling, but for a split second it felt like we were.

Our bodies are wired so that when another body moves we immediately sense their kinesthetic state in our own muscle and breath. It happens instantly, before we can even think about it. Dramatic examples of this include watching an acrobat on a high wire. We tense with the anxiety of falling. At a football game, people contract with the impact on the field, yell, and leap up. My favourite example, though, is how it feels to be in a room of active kids. It doesn't take long to feel over-stimulated.

You plead with them to be quiet, sit still, or go outside. You feel like you are losing your mind. Why? Just standing there, your body is full of their physical energy and cacophony.

Our bodies not only sense the movement of one person, but that of the group. When you enter a room, you receive direct kinesthetic communication from those gathered. Depending on the energy and style of the group communication, you may experience the people as restful, agitated, or engaged. The group body may feel like a good fit or not. This is one way you pick up if you belong.

Similarly, you can sense the movement of animals, earth, and moving objects. When you watch horses run, you identify kinesthetically with their power and freedom. When the world witnessed the World Trade Center towers fall, something inside many of us fell. Similarly, many of us had to stop watching that image when it got too much for us.

You can develop consciousness about what you take in physically and make choices about letting sensations go. You can make choices about the kind of bodyspirits you are around. If you are around energetic, enthusiastic, peaceful bodies, you tend to catch that experience. Just going to the dog park with my dog Christopher moves me to laugh. The carefree, buoyant, rough and tumble freedom of the dogs changes me. Similarly, I choose relationships that offer physical nurture and support. I used to joke that I am such an overly sensitive stress wimp that I had to create InterPlay in order to feel joy at all. Now I see that I created an incredible reservoir of grace in and around me, from which I give generously to the world.

Humans are sensitive. We move each other for better or for worse. When you are with someone who is sick, do you get down? You are moved by their depleted body. You are not separate. When you try to help, you may also be trying to alleviate your own uncomfortable body-to-body feelings. Those of us in helping professions need to be mindful of our kinesthetic awareness. Working with people's dramatic challenges on a daily basis is hard on us. We harden our senses to protect ourselves. This is more than stress. Our compassion muscles are overworked. We can't stop ourselves from picking things up, even if we have good boundaries. We need to move things out and be with bodies that bring us grace.

Even emotion is kinesthetic movement (e-motion). Our body picks up emotional movements, too. I often think of emotion as weather. Feelings are meant to come and go, not get stuck. Letting emotional weather be what it is, letting it storm, shine, breeze, or gust is part of the human package. We can shake out the kinesthetic tensions we pick up, move out the icky stuff through exercise and creativity, and put ourselves in relation to those who are having fun in order to stay in balance.

Dancing is probably one of the fastest and surest ways to clear ourselves from a day of information overload. Dancing involves the big muscles and the subtle, emotional ones. Where exercise at the gym helps us sweat and release tension, it may not help us move our feelings. Music and lyrics give permission to our greater spirit to let more out.

When you feel loaded up or loaded down with life, how do you unload? In InterPlay, exformation is the word we coined to describe moving stuff out of our body, or at least up to our consciousness. A little exformation can relax some people a hundred times faster than getting quiet and centred. Sports, prayer, journalling, and creative expression are powerful, immediate ways to exform. Exformation often involves physically repetitive movements, sounds, actions, or stories and can take many forms: breathing deeply, meditation, physical labour, talking with someone, rocking a child, or hiking. My friend Janie turns Bonnie Raitt music up loud while she enthusiastically irons the altar cloths in the vestry. Beth is a fervent jazzerciser, jumping, sweating, singing, and moving out all the worry she collects. She calls jazzercize her church (her seratonin re-uptake inhibitor, an anti-depressant). George exformed a lot of old fears just by sitting still repeatedly for ten days. His thoughts came and moved on.

PRACTICE: SHAKE OUT WHATEVER YOU'RE SITTING ON
Shake out one hand and then the other. Shake your whole body. Take a deep breath and let it out with a loud sigh. Do it again. For 30 seconds, use sweeping or tossing motions, as though clearing out your space. Throw imaginary paint on the wall. For five seconds, do some fake karate; use your voice as well. If you don't notice any shift, you may need to commit yourself more fully to your movement intention for 30 seconds. Use a little more energy or strength. Take a deep breath and sigh out loud as many times as you need. (Believe me, this is easier to do in a group.)

It can be very difficult to get ourselves to exform at home alone. Being able to find meaningful, affirming community is often the missing motivator needed for releasing, lightening up, and literally coming back to life. Perhaps our bodies know that we need company to help us let go of all that we are carrying. The amazing thing is that moving in community and being witnessed is the fastest, most rewarding way to unclog your spirit pipes. There's a lot to exform and a lot of it is your goodness. So let it go.

Sometimes whole groups need to release their collected kinesthetic tension and information. Three months after the 1989 San Francisco Bay Area earthquake, stories still poured forth between total strangers. "Where were you when it happened?" The whole Bay Area needed to get that quakey, inse-cure movement out. Words and tellings carried the emotion, fear, and energy of that day and gave it back to the outside world. Telling stories of war or of childbirth helps us move accumulated grief, fear, and struggle to the surface.

The good news is that the gift of kinesthetic identification allows us to deeply enjoy, savour, and have our moving world. We experience physical rapport and connection with the crea-tive beauty of our dancing universe, from its most subtle to its grandest physical expression. Even if we only watch from our solo vantage point and barely move at all, we can feel that we are dancing with it all when our kinesthetic sense is involved. Better yet, when we fill with joy, joy starts spontaneously mov-ing out of us. Artists, musicians, poets, and mystics revel in this knowledge. The spontaneous emanations of our bodyspirit are often the most poetic and glorious. Dave Brubeck, musician and composer, said, "How do you imitate God? You create." Improvisers know that creating in the moment is so immedi-ate, so direct and so physical, that it is the most honest prayer there is. In the words of master musician Yehudi Menuin, "Im-provisation is not the expression of accident, but rather of the accumulated yearnings, dreams, and wisdom of our very soul."

You are not required to carry around the experiences of other bodies. You have your life. That's enough. Move experi-ences out of your body.

PLAY: EXFORM AWAY: "OVER THE EDGE," *LIKE BREATHING*, #7
Start a dance with a little shaking of a hand and a deep breath. See where it takes you as you give yourself a chance to release the things that you have stored up.

"I WAS SO DISCONNECTED FROM MY AUTHENTIC SELF THAT I BECAME DEPRESSED."

JANE SIARNY

a self-professed professional dance survivor, had to learn
to dance from the inside out to find real grace.

I came of age in the late 1960s. My world seemed to have the motto, "If you can't say anything nice, don't say anything at all." I stuffed my negative emotions and took on a false "everything's okay" attitude. It was easy to do. I was becoming a good dramatic dancer and could act out characters (mostly happy ones) with no trouble at all. "Everything is beautiful at the ballet." I survived professional dance because I had a supportive and loving family and spouse, the status of a Master of Fine Arts in Dance, and an opportunity to perform. However, even when I moved from ballet to modern and liturgical dance, I was so disconnected from my authentic self that I became depressed.

Everything came crashing down in 1988 when I was 33. Two years prior, my father had committed suicide and after that I was fired from my dream dance company in Chicago. I started therapy and began to untangle the web of denial I had created for myself. My support system expanded to include a committed therapist, the Sacred Dance Guild, and nurturing free-lance dancers in Chicago.

My journey to wholeness was long, confusing, and painful, but I was finally able to affirm and nurture my emerging authentic self. At my first InterPlay retreat in 1994, Cynthia asked me to improvise a solo dance for the community. She challenged me to continue dancing long after I felt that the dance was over.

She asked me to release my performance persona and to dance from within. All of my prior dance education had been focussed on dancing other people's dances, or dancing pure, abstract dances. Who was I in this picture? It was then that I began to strip away the dance that I had borrowed from others to create a new dancing self.

Unfortunately, I thought that I had to give up my technique in order to find my authentic self. I needed to rediscover that I could have technique with authenticity. In my living room, I videotaped myself dancing and played it back while taking on the role of an affirming witness. Witnessing is an integral process in InterPlay, which allows one to be seen, heard, and affirmed by others. I became very compassionate with myself, and inspired to dive down even deeper – to really come home to my bodyspirit.

Playing fueled my desire to move, to be moved, and to have my technique and performance – all the while laying the foundation, a safe place to nurture my emerging authentic self. Things moved along splendidly for six years. I began to teach and perform again with relatively no pain from chronic injuries, which had resulted from so many years of dancing. It wasn't until I adopted my son, however, that I was faced with my biggest challenge. I had overcome so much and had started to grow into the person I wanted to be. Why couldn't I practice affirmation and experience a life full of joy at home? I wanted to play with my son – really play like we do in InterPlay. I wanted to become so ever-present to the moment, letting go of expectations and judgments.

I often flash back to my childhood. By the age of five, I was dancing everywhere – the backyard, the driveway, the garage. I soon learned that dancing is more properly done in the dance studio, on the stage, or in the living room (if you are practicing or performing for your family). But now my practice is to be open to the dance everywhere – finding those places in my life where I can truly be spontaneous, confident, joyful, and free. Like any artistic or spiritual discipline, it takes constant practice.

I know that caring for my four-year-old is a gift of grace in my life. So many people tell me that in a wink of an eye it will be over. He has so many lessons to teach me. Am I open to learning about the grace that comes from really living a life based in affirmation? Most of the new parenting books advocate this. Don't dwell on the negative behaviour. Look for the good. Children have an inherent desire to please and to be co-operative. If it works for my child, can it also work for the other relationships in my life? I still desire to change and to be more present to this world but I'm less inclined to fix things now. I get more energy from seeing what is there to be celebrated and affirmed.

When I was so cut off from myself and escaped into dance, I used to pray that I would be a real person someday – have friends outside of dance, have a child, feel connected to the world. It was something like Gepeto's prayer in the movie *Pinocchio*: "If only you were a real boy." My blue fairy came to me in the form of InterPlay. And like Pinocchio, I dove into the deep ocean, wrestled with the whale and the waves, and landed on the shore. I dance for joy.

12

CHOOSING
TOUCH

One January in Australia, I received a massage from a friend. My face ached like a parched desert that hadn't seen rain in eons. I took my masseuse's hands and pushed them into my cheeks and eyes. It was like drinking from a well. My tears flowed. After the masseuse left, I had a remarkable sense that Christ came, embraced and kissed me all over. It had never occurred to me that a relationship with the holy would come directly through sensuality. In the muted light, I realized that if the holy could love me like this, then nothing was wrong with my sensual body. Sensuality is a source from which to draw spiritual support. When I rose from the table, I was surprised to feel the palms of my hands. They were sensing and awake, like a blind person gaining sight for the first time. Energy filled my hands and they were ravenous for contact. Home from Australia, the first thing I did was to enroll in a three-week course, led by MaryAnn Finch, called "Massage: the Art of Anointing," in order to feast on contact, mutuality, and joy.

Moving hands are open channels for grace and life. Through them you are meant to be nourished and blessed. This is a far cry from the parental message, "Keep your hands to yourself" – a lesson we may have learned too well.

PRACTICE: LET TOUCH IN

Bring your palms together. Instead of touching to feel things, feel the simplicity of this basic sense of your hands as they touch. Notice temperature, texture, and pressure. Savour sensation, as if enjoying a nutritious meal. Touch different things. Let your hand simply rest on something. Sense differences in energy, heat, or texture. Notice what you enjoy.

PARTNERED PLAY: FAKE MASSAGE

With a friend or pet, experiment with "fake" massage. "Fake massage" releases us from our pictures of meaningful and healing touch, and allows us to experiment with what our sense of touch is asking for or saying in the present moment. Lay your hands on your partner's back, listening to your own tactile desires. Release yourself from obligations to help or give to your partner if you can, and allow yourself just to have contact. Follow the pleasure of your hands whether still, light, playful, or gently forceful. Or you may even find your hands lifting off the body altogether. That is fine. Delighting in your own touch paradoxically opens the way to a wondrous experience of receiving for your partner. Our own gifts of healing touch may flourish when we give ourselves permission to listen to our own senses. Wouldn't you like to know that someone massaging you was also receiving from the experience?

This kind of fake, non-technical massage satisfies both parties. Like easy focus in the eyes, easy hands move beyond the physical dualities of giving and receiving, to the greater state of having contact. It is a shared experience. Our own needs access our unique gift of touch. Touch that isn't focussed on healing or changing people engages our creative energy. And this is powerful.

Jo Lin was in touch with his body wisdom at the wedding of two special friends from East Timor. The militia and Indonesian military had ransacked almost all the towns and villages and had killed many innocent people. Jo recalled: "Constantino, who had suffered greatly under the Indonesian occupation, brought a severe migraine to his wedding. I was asked to apply heat to his temples using moxibustion with a thick burning incense-like stick. The heat seemed to be useful in dilating the blood vessels, but I sensed that I should also cradle his head in my hands... Constantino fell into a deep restful sleep. He felt the headache lift. He said I was a healer. But I say he and Inge, his wife, are heroes!"

Touch is a communal, familial, spiritual form. In Thailand, massage is practiced on Buddhist temple grounds and is integral to the lives of priests. Laying on of hands in baptism, prayer, sickness, death, ordination, and anointing are central to Christian practice. The power to communicate spirit is literally in the touch, not just the symbol of it. Through simple touch Jesus often healed people and told his disciples they would do the same. Sacred touch is a holy signature of the life-giving power of human contact.

Reintroducing physical contact in a playful community opens the windows and doors of spirit, energy, and joy. So simple, the direct touch of hand to hand, or shoulder to shoulder is an immediate tonic to isolation and tension. Jake Empereur, my Catholic seminary professor, instituted ballroom dance classes for priests and nuns on sabbatical. He knew the challenges of celibacy and sacrificial vocational pursuit. He also knew that the lack of fun and healthy contact were dehumanizing. His classes were full.

The most direct way to cross social thresholds is the handshake. It involves both touch and movement, and communicates greeting, agreement, and friendship. Taking the handshake one small but mighty step further, we can access a world of communion that touch offers while maintaining our social bearings.

PARTNERED PRACTICE: PALM-TO-PALM CONTACT
WITH A PARTNER

Bring your hand to a partner's hand.

Push. Give each other a push to feel your strength and theirs.

Lean away. Grab wrists and lean back sensing the shared weight and solidity between your bodies.

Come back up to standing.

Reshape your palms. Change the palm-to-palm connection to a new shape.

Be still. Hold the shape briefly and enjoy the stillness.

Change quickly from shape to shape, going faster than the speed of your mind. Flow with the contact. Palm to palm, follow the moving connection. If standing, release your feet from their place, allowing the hands to lead you beyond your spot.

Drop contact. Step back from your partner. Open the space between the hands while maintaining the sense of connection over several yards. Drop your hands and let go of connection. Put hands up and reestablish contact across the distance. No contact is a necessary choice.

PARTNERED PLAY: HAND-TO-HAND DANCE: "ON BEHALF OF,"
***LIKE BREATHING* #14**

Using some of the basic vocabulary for a dance of contact – push, pull, changing shapes, being still, moving together, coming apart and back together – with music, follow the connection. Experiment with the dance as it comes. Once you get going, it's good to trick your partner a little. Keep your sense of humour. See what you notice.

———

After dancing like this, one woman said, "I've lived most of my life behind such strong, rigid barriers that even though I see and know intellectually others are friends, I continue to struggle with the fear of reaching out. But when I am relaxed I am able to directly sense things in others; somehow I just feel things about the relationship...and on days that I have contact with other people I feel better. Contact improvisation gives me energy I hunger for and unfortunately fear."

The relational truths that emerge from making contact are powerful. We don't seem to realize that our ability to trust, feel safe, or be spontaneous with others is ultimately rooted in how our bodies work. But it is all right there. Playing with a perfect stranger can feel like finding a long-lost friend. A long-term relationship in which we have not yet learned to dance may be the most complex, physically challenging dance of all. Katrina Browne, social activist and filmmaker, found herself delightfully undone by direct physical play. After dancing in contact, Katrina wrote this poem entitled *Contact Duet*.

I.

five minutes of slow intimate toes
am I looking for love
simplicity
or best friend age ten?
so much right here in my own backyard

II.
may I know your ankle?
may I tread lightly on your skin?
on your particular hairs issuing forth from your particular
ankle's skin?
generous skin.
suddenly, we're a monument, felt:
four feet balanced as high
as anything
ever
was

Letting your body grow hospitable to human contact makes you softer, warmer, more alive and accessible in community. Bump into someone on the street, in an elevator, or inadvertently touch a friend, and the first word that comes out is usually, "Sorry." But walk, stop, or run with a room full of people with everyone narrowly missing each other, even walking backwards, and the laughter heightens. If you bump into someone, just say "thank you." When it is fun and not made too big a deal of, it gets easier and easier to make contact in community.

———

PRACTICE: "THANK YOU" INSTEAD OF "SORRY"

Today, when you accidentally make contact with people, imagine saying, "Thank you" instead of "I'm sorry."

———

Groups that include healthy touch can have stronger connections. Hospital chaplain Jurgen Schwing craves tangible support in his community, saying

When push comes to shove
I love it.
Pushing, pulling, leaning, lifting.
Shoving, roughing, having, releasing.
I want a community
to push up against.

Sleep-overs, camping, dance parties, mosh pits, and just hanging out together bring us into contact when we are young. As we age, we're supposed to couple up, have children, and get our needs for contact met privately. If only half of us are in committed relationships at any time, primary sexual relationships can't be a full replacement for our need for communal affection. Most of us are starving and we don't even know it. Holding hands is wonderful. But what about our deeper hungers for contact?

———

PARTNERED PLAY: LEANING: "TURBAN BLUES,"
***LIKE BREATHING*, #18**

Sit side by side with another person and lean into them. As you lean, hold to the centre of your own body. Once you can feel where you are in the lean, relax your muscles and let go into the resting place between your bodies. Lean in. Play with a dance of leaning in and away.

———

Dr. Martin Kelly lives with the Pitjantjatjara people in central Australia. One of his most vivid memories occurred during the accidental death of a young girl he had befriended. He did everything to save her, but couldn't. When her mother arrived, she would not come in to look upon her dead child. Martin went outside the clinic and the mother crumpled in his arms.

Together they fell to their knees in grief. That evening a "sorry camp" was made in the desert. The community built fires, brought food, and with no words but hushed whispers and crying, drew close. Martin, too, the white doctor who failed to save the child, was held and embraced. Children, young men, and women came to him, sat in his lap and wept with him. Communal silence and contact carried them through the first comfortless days.

Leaning offers one set of lessons. Leveraging and lifting another body offers other uncommon wisdom. It was not until I was in my 30s that I learned that even at 135 pounds I could lift a man heavier than me. I found I had strength to literally push and pull my own weight in relationships, and that tenderness was only part of my feminine vocabulary. It would have been wonderful to have known this sooner. Not that I need to be a "pushy broad." It is more that I have found greater inner security as I have learned how strong and capable I am.

Lifting each other creates a camaraderie of flight and power in us. Diane Rawlinson, an outstanding high school dance teacher, wrote to me once to share what a great day she had with her students:

...even had the guys lifting, leaning, pushing, supporting, etc. and just enjoying working with one another. When it was over they were "high-fiving" each other. Then, I picked one kid to improv with me who I knew could make the jump from student/teacher to just two bodies dancing together. It was freeing for me. The students enjoyed witnessing it too. They got to see me dance beyond teaching. Given the whole issue of no physical contact between teachers and students it was a big step, but we discussed that too. What an amazing day!

The power of touch is a possible, life-changing, and immediate choice. The more we have contact in healthy community the more grace we have. In times when unhealthy touch wins the headlines, playing with healthy contact is more needed than ever. Even a hand on a shoulder is a moment of grace. Rules can't protect us from sexual harm if we don't get enough affection in the first place. After years of paying attention to the skin hunger in bodies all around me, I read a newspaper article about a school prohibiting teenagers from hugging. My reaction was to write this poem.

Even a finger to a knee
and you break
the surface tension between bodies.
Don't you know
13-year-olds need to hug,
old people need their children to crawl
into bed with them,
and dying mothers
and men, especially men,
just need to have their
hands held?

———

"I AM A CARE-GIVING GURU WHO USED TO BE UNABLE TO RECEIVE."

———

ROD PATTENDEN

Australian curator, artist, and minister, recovered his lost joy in caring through physical contact in community.

I thought I would lose myself, and yet I most truly wanted to. I had become boring and predictable, facing early middle age with few resources, except for the habit of turning up each day with my clothes and smile worn well. Dance and improvisation would surely expose me. I would lose control. I might be seen for what I was – a body craving touch, affirmation, and reassurance. The last and the best place I wanted to be seen like this was in an InterPlay class!

Previously I had developed habits of working too hard, of taking no time for pleasure, and of focussing on things that were serious and that served the needs of others. InterPlay looked frivolous and dangerous. Here were people inventively playing their way through space with obvious pleasure. And yet as I began to let go of my fears, I surprisingly found myself. Making contact with other bodies has proven to be a wonderful way to come home to myself as a gracious and alive person.

I have thrived on gaining access to the strength, support, and trust of other embodied persons. I am not a person alone, but one who can give and receive trust, support, and loving affirmation. People no longer just need me for my place in the work or food chain, but for the delightful sense of enjoying me. I like leaning into another body, taking myself off the centre point of stable gravity, and sensing a reciprocal sense of support. It is exhilarating, as most of the time in my family and workplace, I feel like I am alone, struggling with the system that is supposed to be nurturing us all. I am the worried mother, fussing all the time! It is such pleasure to instead be there with other bodies, to play with and to receive their gifts.

In my life, I lead a small organization, I am the oldest in my family of siblings, and I have compassion fatigue in my close relationships. I am a care-giving guru who used to be unable to receive. I never made time to hang around other people just for fun. Making contact has provided me with the most immediate and intimate ways of being found in community, through delight rather than through a role.

The permission to push has been of particular significance. To push into another body, as I feel their trust and balance, is an experience at the cellular level that has been ecstatically transforming. In all the other areas of my life, I have trained to hold myself back. To worry about the other person in case I knock them over, or frighten them, or overwhelm them. Better be quiet, check out the scene, fit in, all good counsellor training – advanced empathy, a great prescription for dumb absence and the loneliness of life. Pushing into someone else's strength, creativity, and laughter enables me to celebrate my own capacities and, more importantly, my desires. I can listen for what I want in this moment and not put it off. Today I need more support, thank you. A little affirmation over there would be nice, and a side-serve of strange, comic irony would round off a nourishing meal, thank you. Oh, and I would like it all served on a platter of outrageous laughter. Delicious!

Knowing myself in desire, fear, hope, and fragility, grounds me in a way that I have become more hospitable to the presence of others different from me. Rather than manipulating situations and people out of fear to conform to my expectations, I now feel comfortable to be surprised and interested in the uniqueness and difference of others.

My leadership style has also changed. I expect those I work with to be able to be present with more of themselves, rather than the thin surface of their presentation. We value and enjoy our strengths and amaze ourselves that we are able to produce more together than we can as individuals. I tend not to hold back. I thrust my energy and desire out into the space, looking for playmates and collaborators, knowing that in a complex dance, I work better and enjoy myself more.

This gift of making contact with other people teaches me to respect the boundaries of others. It reminds me of the continual surprise found in human bodies across cultures, races, and gender. This strange diversity also brings the ability to celebrate my own uniqueness and not to apologize in any way for my own presence. In losing myself in this way, I have found myself, and I have to confess that I am beginning to like, live with, and even enjoy what I have found!

WHEN LIFE DRIVES YOU OUT OF YOUR MIND, ENJOY THE RIDE

BODY INTELLECTUALS

13

TAKING YOUR MENTAL LID OFF

I stand in front of grown adults and ask them to put their hands on top of their heads like a lid. When all 30 of us are standing with a hand on our crown, we make a squeaking sound like a rusty hinge and open the lid. Eeeeeeeeeech. People can't help laughing.

"What did you think getting out of your head would be like?" I ask. For one split second, the idea that healing the split between your physicality and intellect might be fun is startling. Instead of shaming ourselves for lack of concentration, loss of conscious memory, and catastrophic thinking, we crack open our mind, air it out, and let it be.

It turns out that we hold our minds in too-small a physical space, a box the size of a skull. To think outside of the box, you've got to let your mind be as big as your bodyspirit. Your mind wants to play. Your mind wants to move around, engage, and gad about with insatiable curiosity. Your mind wants to be as big as you are. Let your mind go! Let your mind grow! Let it be big.

PRACTICE: OPEN UP THAT HEAD SPACE

Shake out your arms. Shake out your voice. Shake out your head. Take some deep breaths. Open your face as wide as you can and squinch it up. Massage your face. What is the first thing you notice?

If it takes you a moment to notice anything, that is a good sign. Your "focusser" is relaxed. Your mind is bigger now, more open, receptive. An open mind may feel as if no sensations, no stressors at all are pulling or calling for attention. This state, cherished in both religious and academic practices, is called an open mind, beginners mind, or no mind.

An open mind is full of ambiguity. It dances with many things. Thoughts, reactions, sensations, and imaginings constantly come and go. Confusion occurs as opposite ideas fuse or meld together. "I love you, but I don't want to be hurt by you." "I want it and I don't." Among the many choices occurring in the complexity of life, we vacillate from thought to thought. We want to take a stand, to feel clear and firm in ourselves. We could just say, "I am thinking about it." But we don't. More often, we follow a group belief or higher authority as a guidepost. It's easier.

Ambiguity means "to move around between." I believe our intolerance of ambiguity in life is literally a result of separating our body movement from our thinking and our spirit. When we put mind and spirit in boxes, it is as if they shrink and detach from the amazing fullness of our experience. Our mind physically narrows, our spirit floats around somewhere, and our bodies are left behind frustrated and confused.

We are used to keeping a lid on our minds. Fearing judgment, we withhold the expression of our thoughts and ideas. I used to feel the heat and sweat of the adrenal stress when I had an idea rise up during a lecture in college. My heart would palpitate at the thought of speaking up. When this happened, I knew I really had something to contribute. My hand would go up, but the act of thinking out loud in public nearly overwhelmed me.

PRACTICE: TAKE YOUR MENTAL LID OFF

Using your kinesthetic imagination, put your hand on top of your head like a lid. Make a sound like a rusty hinge as you take your lid off. Grab hold of whatever is under wraps and fling it in the air.

Wheeeeee! Do this until you feel less mental.

Moving and thinking are really all we ever do. In spite of the left brain-right brain theory, we think and feel simultaneously as we drive, walk, shop, make love, work out at the gym, or practice law. People report that their best ideas come while moving around. Our mind goes places. We think about work while playing golf. We golf while we are thinking about a project. When your bodymind works in concert, there is an ease and grace that is discernible. Ideas pop. New connections are made.

PRACTICE: FASTER THAN THE SPEED OF THOUGHT

Put your hand in the air. Hold it in position. Change it to a different position. Change it again. Each time you change create a distinct shape. Now change shapes faster than the speed of your mind.

The way we normally think of thinking, as focussed analysis or study, is only one of the ways that our minds move. Critical thinking and reasoning are isolated movement tasks. While extremely valuable on their own, we can learn to have this skill in partnership with the greater dance of the mind. As you dance your mind, you will hardly believe all that you become. The integrated thoughtfulness of our entire physical system working as a whole is wondrously healing. It changes everything. It is radiant and opens new vistas.

———

"MY SUCCESS WAS TO GET OUT OF MY HEAD AND INTO MY BODY."

———

WILLIAM FROST

William Frost's divorce was a turning point. A change of mind was not enough to help him find peace.

In the autumn of 1999, after 18 years of marriage and three wonderful boys, my wife informed me that she was leaving me, that she needed to "experience her independence." Shocked into awakening, and desperate to not "be left" or to admit defeat, I immediately made numerous lifestyle changes towards which I had been stubbornly dragging my feet. The changes seemed to make a difference and brought about temporary hopefulness. A few weeks later, however, it was revealed that my wife's "independence" also included her desire to have a relationship with her art teacher. She claimed that she did not actually want to leave me, but believed that I would not be able to allow room in our relationship for her to experience her relationship with him as well. Clearly, if I were going to accept this aspect, it was going to take me to a greater level of transformation than I was prepared for (no matter how creative or willful I believed my-self to be).

Being a consummate competitor, a lifelong "jock," and ex-tensively trained in creative problemsolving skills, I became determined to "change my mind," to literally reprogram my neurological patterns of conditioned, fear-based thinking in order to make room in my mind for my wife to have her inde-pendence without having to leave me. What I did not realize at the time was that I was attempting to do something that was not right for me, not right for my heart. I did not want to be in a polyamorous relationship, but out of shame and guilt, the obvious challenge to my competitive nature, the desire to keep my family close together and a disproportionate desire to please, I began frantically trying to convince myself that an "open marriage" could work.

Over the next several months I put into practice every crea-tivity technique I had ever learned, taught, or facilitated for oth-ers; I used guided imagery tapes, prayer, meditation, labyrinth walking, journalling, inspirational and enlightening readings, empowerment exercises, and healing affirmations. Sometimes I wrote stream-of-consciousness outpourings that lasted the entire night. Over time, I convinced myself that I could accept this new man and the changes I would have to make. But it was a delusion. It wasn't real. It wasn't sustainable. And deep inside, it was killing me. As the frequency and spirit of my wife's new relationship grew, I became more and more aware that it was taking a toll on my body. I was experiencing aches and pains in my upper back, a fairly regular pain in my left shoulder, and my heart often hurt so much I thought I was having a series of minor heart attacks.

Nothing helped. Not ibuprofen, nor Shiatsu massage, visualizations, therapy, or acupuncture. It wasn't until midsum-mer of the following year, when my good friend Peter encour-aged me to join a group of InterPlayers, that I finally began to experience some relief. And I finally came to understand that the missing link in my attempts to move through the pain of my broken relationship was the changing of my cellular memory to go along with the changing of my neurological memory. What I realized through many sessions of movement and play was that the most important creative technique for my success was to get out of my head and into my body.

InterPlay was the first "tool" I had ever experienced where the intention promoted awareness of both the kinesthetic processes and the cognitive processes of change. It was a place where graceful flowing movements could coexist with athleticism, and novel ideas could flow naturally without use of fancy techniques. It was a place where I could quiet the incessant chatter of my busy mind and simply listen to the wisdom of what my body was trying to tell me. Immersing myself in InterPlay facilitated moving my body and finding my voice in ways that allowed my emotions to move through me, rather than remain blocked. In my attempt to approach my crisis situation in what I believed to be an "enlightened" way, I had unwittingly stored up a great deal of unexpressed grief.

Through InterPlay, I have been able to accept and express that grief. I have become able to tell the truth, to release the secrets that have bound me in shame for a lifetime. I am more self-accepting, less ruled by my competition and performance orientation, and have been able to let go of my marriage and the desperate need to be loved. I have learned to move in ways that swell up from an authentic inner rhythm rather than from any artificial external source.

My new-found dancing and storytelling has brought me untold grace, peace, and a loving community. I have cultured a greater ability to be present and to listen to the truth within me. In a very real way, InterPlay has changed my mind, changed my body, and saved my life.

14

LIBERATING A MADE-UP MIND

I admire people who have been trained to think in a certain way for countless years, and then to their own surprise, and everyone else's, they suddenly shift or move on. Pat Pothier, a retired psychiatric nursing professor, is one of these people. She began to dance improvisationally in her 70s. She writes about her liberation from set patterns in her poem *Overcoming the Tyranny of External Information*.

As I walk into the room,
The door slams shut behind me.

The darkened room in front of me is filled
With red day-glo signs.

DON'T / STOP
SHOULD / NO

SHOULD NOT
BE QUIET/BE GOOD
DON'T MOVE/DON'T MOVE
DON'T BREATHE

What are the consequences of not obeying?
A sign in bold black letters informs.

ABANDONMENT

Seventy years later
I open the door and
Dance
Into the sunlight.

A FREE WOMAN!

Pat Pothier has a dancing mind, a mind that is not stuck but that can move.

It is easy to lose ourselves and our freedom to the rigidity of a technique, structure, or belief system. Minds that hold tight have difficulty finding grace. Many theologians and psychologists have observed that, in this way, the mind is an obstacle to grace. Insisting on one way negates the very foundation of a moving life. In the aftermath of the September 11 terrorist attacks on the United States, I am even more aware of the dangers of the all-or-nothing approach.

On the other hand, a playful, open, dancing mind actually believes that movement, change, and mystery are fundamental to experience. Even God, Divine Mind, can move and change, as is depicted in biblical story after story. Prophets from Moses to Jesus talk to God to sway and change the course of events.

God is influenced and therefore changed. God's mind moves. Dancing minds can believe what they believe and still have room for ideas to live, move, grow, and transform.

Appreciating and realizing that minds move is a signature of the dance of life. If we are to structure our recurring thoughts, wisdom, and experiences into beliefs, we need beliefs that respect how the body actually works. We need beliefs that dance. We need laughing, crying minds; the kind of minds implied by G. K. Chesterton's famous quote: "Probably the reason angels can fly is because they take themselves lightly." To laugh is to dance with our mind, to stay loose and let truth surprise and shake us. Laughter literally shakes out our brains!

PRACTICE: YAWN AND CHUCKLE

Experiment for ten seconds each with these physical exercises for your head and see what you notice. Yawn for ten seconds. Open your face really wide and then squinch it up. Move your face to the right and then to the left and then all around. Don't look in the mirror! One friend, a professor, was surprised that he looked like a pirate in the mirror! Now do a little fake chuckling. For ten seconds, repeat the sound of hee hee hee hee. Then repeat the sound of ha ha ha ha. Last, repeat the sound of ho ho ho ho. What do you notice about your head?

Intelligence is a whole, joyous, creative, energetic, physical act. Creative thinkers know this. They pay attention as thoughts incrementally evolve, swirl, thrust, and hang. They love to compose, sense sequence and pattern, leap toward barely felt images, let ideas pop, and marvel at the detail and dimension in an already elucidated idea. The freer we are to dance our thoughts, the more we come to our genius.

JOURNAL: NOTICE YOUR THOUGHTS MOVE

In stillness, observe your thoughts for one minute. Remember that they are physicalities. They may feel so much like "you" that you don't notice them like you notice a feeling. Watch them move from thing to thing. Jot down thoughts you recall.

———

I've discovered that our thoughts move incredibly fast. In the space of 30 seconds, I notice my painted table across the room, and the guitar which makes me think of my daughter and her horseback lessons. The clock ticks and evokes the thought of time passing. I suddenly think of needing to do the dishes and then I feel hunger pangs and wonder if I need to eat.

PLAY: DANCE WITH ONE HAND, LET YOUR MIND FOLLOW:
"LIKE BREATHING," *LIKE BREATHING*, #2

Raise a hand in the air to begin, starting with slow and smooth movements. Play with any dynamics or energy you feel in your body right now. Notice your mind. Does it follow the dance or try to lead it? Can you let your mind follow the movement?

———

Many people discover that their mind becomes quiet when they move. Some say the mind is a monkey that will follow any passing fancy. I say the mind is a dancer going with the music of the moment, sometimes leading, sometimes following.

I don't think we want to have minds that are fixated and static. This can even be considered dangerous or obsessive. Holding onto our ideas, our ideals, our images, or our desires creates physical fatigue.

———

PRACTICE: HOLD IT!

Clench your fist for 30 seconds. Notice the effect on your hand, your arm, and the rest of your body. Hold out your arm or stand on one leg. Hold your position. How long can you do it? What happens to you physically?

———

When you hold a position indefinitely, gravity seems to intensify, fatigue increases, and eventually you fall. Your position becomes precarious because this is the way nature works. (I love the thought that, etymologically speaking, precarious originally meant "dependent on prayer.") The mind is physical. It's a dancer that requires movement, breath, and flexibility. Make up your mind for good and before long you will be on your knees and sorry that you were so sure of yourself.

Since the mind is embodied, it follows physical rules. The mind cannot hold anything indefinitely. Even people with good ideas corrupt them with dogmatic holding, and those who mentally have fallen way off balance can get up. Physical impermanence is good news. As my poem says,

> A body cannot hold a position forever.
> But torture asks us to.
> So does belief, but a body
> cannot hold a position forever.
>
> Gravity will break us down
> trembling muscle,
> or a hand lift us up
> in blessing from above,
> but a body cannot
> hold a position forever.

Tortured or torturer, no matter.
The painful release of wrong action
will come. Sin will fall away.
Evil will pass. It's a fact,
a body cannot hold
a position forever.
Not even beauty and good.
You can try to hold on.
Or you can prepare to let go.

Classical religions offer clues about having dancing beliefs. Buddhism practices detachment from thought, and enables practitioners to touch a deep stream of peace. Counteracting the temptation to then resist thought, sensation, and emotion, Zen Buddhism was created to shake up attempts to do things right.

Christ offered forgiveness as a way to keep us from getting stuck in belief. To detach from dogmatic self-righteousness, healthy Christian practitioners let go of unilateral ideas that hold us apart from reuniting with those who have hurt us. Forgiveness (giving as we gave before we were hurt), going back to God's original playground where we can experience life giving itself to us again, restores us to the creative freedom and generative love of the divine universe. This is the dance that no idea or belief can measure up to.

Theologian Robert McAfee Brown's mind might have been a Baryshnikov of the mind. Jailed as a Freedom Rider during the Civil Rights movement, he protested military involvement in Vietnam and Central America, and worked for inter-religious dialogue. His theological commitments were embodied in his actions. At his retirement party, he fulfilled a dream of performing a cello piece that had been played at Auschwitz. To do this, he had to learn cello at age 70 and be willing to play the piece at his own level. At the party, he also invited a dance on homelessness, shared one of his most notorious limericks, and honoured the receptionist as the person most deserving of recognition. His playful mind was embodied, humble and free, lined up to bless us all, as it says in James 1:22–25: "Be doers of the word, and not merely hearers who deceive themselves… [for] those who look into the perfect law, the law of liberty, and persevere, being not hearers who forget but doers who act – they will be blessed in their doing."

When it comes down to it, the mind is the biggest dancer of all. Thought is always on the move. A gracious mind must learn to simultaneously let go and hold on like a trained dancer.

———

"IF I DON'T GET OVER MY JUDGMENTS, I MIGHT
SUFFOCATE AND DIE (A TRAGIC AND UNNECESSARY
DEATH) BEFORE OUR FIRST SHOW."

LEAH MANN

a creative thinker and performer, battles between a perfectionist
drive and a joy that is determined to get her thoughts to cha-cha,
samba, swing, and waltz.

Interesting world I've entered, the Oregon Country Fair, the
first stop of our touring season – Hippie City, USA. We are
greeted by very happy hairy people, waving, dancing around,
and pointing us to the various necessary destinations – regis-
tration, backstage, and campground. It's like we've entered a
funky funky version of Walmart! I think to myself that I don't
like what either are "selling" or "free-trading."

I begin to contract, stable data being tweaked, wanting to
separate myself from "them." I shout in mind, "I am different
than you! I am 'righter' than you! I used to teach drug and preg-
nancy prevention to youth! I don't drink and I don't do drugs!
Free love is a myth that brings greater heartache! And don't
you see that I am better than you! I need no substances, I just
'trip' on myself!"

This is the come-as-you-are church. Barefooted, bare-
chested, bare bottomed, bear costumed; fully dragged, solar
powered, highly stilted or just high; red, yellow, black, brown,
white, purple or blue; tattooed, glittered, henna'd or bindi'd;
every shape, size, and age seeking authenticity and a place to
express it fully, I realize that some prophetic hippie foretold this
moment with the invention of the word "uptight." I am holding my breath. If I don't get over my judgments, I might suffocate and die (a tragic and unnecessary death) before our first

show.

In the midst of this, I recall that I have been trying to incorporate more "swing" into my life. Swing is the effort of relaxation, going with the flow, inhale / exhale, rocking, swaying, releasing. Riding the swing of my mood, I realize "I am a thirsty person in the rain!" I am in the land of swing… why do you think they call them hippies?!

I decide I should take notes, from the experts.

1. A circle always works better than a hierarchy in the happiness arena. Here everyone circles around creativity – crafts, visual and performing arts. It's a highly functioning body in which the head acknowledges the equal importance of the spine or the trash emptier or the sauna stoker. (Isn't that biblical?) People make the pilgrimage from all over the world just to be part of the manifested organism of the fair.

2. Everyone is naked under their clothes. Why all the shame? It isn't really "sexy" but it sure is simple and, well…natural!

3. Some use water for baptism, but at the Country Fair, dirt is the element to ceremoniously acknowledge one's connection to the divine.

4. Organized hippy (or swinger for that matter) is not an oxymoron.

5. It's better to not look back when leaving Sodom, better known as the "port o' lets." Let go, release, and relieve yourself! Leave the poop behind!

6. Sharing is good. Need a light, need a food voucher, need a towel, need a drink of water? Need a hug? Just ask and witness lots of gratefulness on both sides .

7. Miracles abound. I don't know much about the Grateful Dead, but apparently folks used to wait outside the sold-out concerts with signs that said, "I need a miracle" and people would just up and give them their miracle – free

tickets. The same occurs at this fair, which reaches its capacity, allowing only ticket holders to enter. Miracles could happen more if we let our community know our needs and desires.

8. And finally, just because someone else is not resonating with my authenticity, it doesn't mean that I should stifle myself. Be bold, be absolute, be true!

The highlight of the fair was experiencing the over 3,000 people standing and cheering for our unique genre of work. We don't fit into any category easily. It's dance, it's music, it's the animation of large kinetic sculptures, it's theatre, it's improv, it's play, all happening simultaneously. And as we'd walk through the paths to and from our shows, people would yell from their booths or call to us as we passed, "We dig your work, Lelavision!" "You rock!" "Totally awesome show!" "I love you!" And I realize I like this "free love" idea. What affirmations have I forgotten to give?

On this opening gig of our tour, on this initiation of our gypsy-hood for the next five months, I learned a song in a sauna with 50 sweaty naked people. It's our theme song now, our prayer to God, and how we'd like to carry the Holy Spirit with us as creative spark and play to every place we land.

> Lightly touch down
> To earth and ocean,
> Sand and sea
> Wind in motion
> Fire ignite in me
> In me Spirit ignite in me.

Now for something completely different…next stop, the Quaker Church in Edinburgh!

15

BECOMING A BODY INTELLECTUAL

At an academic conference, Phil invited the assembly to "Raise your hand if you are an intellectual." A hand or two went up. It was a timid response for such an intellectually gifted crowd. I don't think they had ever been asked the question before or been invited to publicly claim it. Claiming our intellect is much like claiming to be an artist. It's not something you talk about even if you've dedicated your life to ideas.

I have come timidly into claiming my love of intellectual life. Is it because I come from a family where intellectualism is uncommon? Is it because as a dancer it is more difficult for me or other people to recognize the nature of my ideas? I don't know, but I have had to make it a spiritual discipline just to call myself an intellectual. Even so, I am not a sit-in-the-library, lab, or café intellectual. My intellectual curiosity is inseparable from the world of action and physicality. Phil and I coined the term "body intellectual" to describe the wholeness of our intellectual activities. People often laugh when we use this term. Together, these words seem like opposites.

Body intellectuals are those who can dance with their mind and be mindful about the dance of their lives. Body intellectuals are experts at noticing, responding to, and articulating the way their whole bodies work. We body intellectuals seek to understand how individual, communal, and earth life works best in practical terms.

Phil and I wanted a system of thoughts that could articulate and embrace our physically integrated approach. The history and language that continuously splits spirit and mind from the body made it necessary to reconstruct the platform of principles and a way of talking that affirmed thinking as whole beings. We wanted language that directly supported and affirmed our experiences of whole-body freedom in InterPlay. We wanted a universal place of articulation where people from different religions could identify with the simple, physically rooted, life-affirming ideas. After lots of play, Phil and I created ten Body Wisdom Principles on our first lap top computer. Sitting by a pool in Hawaii, we brainstormed words and phrases about what we knew. Then we agreed to explain ourselves using brief, simple, concise language. We committed to staying away from theologically and philosophically cumbersome words. These are the ten principles that emerged.

1. Mind body heart and spirit are one. Physicality is basic.
2. You don't have to articulate your experience in order to have it.
3. Grace is physical. We receive, send, create, and have it in body.
4. We can notice the details (body data) and patterns (body knowledge) in our experience and make wise choices (body wisdom) for our own good and that of all creation.

5. Compassion is kinesthetic. When one body suffers, everybody suffers.
6. Personal body knowledge is authoritative and can be trusted.
7. Exform. Bodies need to get rid of stuff we collect.
8. Through body wisdom, we can expand our present time to be spacious and fun.
9. Play is easier on the body than work. An ethic of play keeps us at our best.
10. Looking for the good in life is more fun that looking for the bad. Affirm Life.

All of these ideas took their impulse from embracing a physicality of grace rather than struggle. Instead of attempting to control the body, we eagerly listened for and acted on the wisdom of our bodies, and that of other bodies. We valued and affirmed our inner authority as well as the authority of the community.

Thinking with the whole body and not in spite of it has resulted in greater health for me and many others. Health honours our createdness as central to the whole human enterprise. Instead of feeling shame about humanness, we more easily embrace our limits and move toward our strengths.

I am proud of a great deal of mentoring I received in the Christian tradition that has affirmed physicality and the incarnation of Love. I found many people who said "Yes" to embodied spirituality, if not in words then in practice. In my early 20s, the Benedictine monks of St. Andrew's Priory showed me in dramatic and playful ways that being human is good. At a dance workshop at their priory in the middle of the Southern California desert, our retreat director proposed an improvisational foot wrestling contest with one of the brown-robed brothers. I came from my corner of the ring on all fours crawling like a crab toward my opponent, a Benedictine brother, our feet and toes bared for the contest. Afterward, we picnicked at nearby Devil's Punch Bowl State Park, where Bud Light and laughter made it even clearer that love of God and open fun were not mutually exclusive. I felt I knew these people as people and not just as monks.

Personal principles don't replace traditional wisdom. I believe traditions were once and can still be body wisdom. Unlike tradition, however, your own principles validate the role of personal truth, cultural evolution, and body wisdom-in-the-making. As we build up more grace in the world, our own beliefs are a vital and unreplaceable contribution to the process.

Create your own principles. Noticing certain things to be consistently true over time, you can find your own credo of experience.

JOURNAL: BRAINSTORM YOUR BODY-BASED WISDOM

Make a short list of things you know from your own experience. If it is hard to get started, use a subject to give you a focus. For instance, what do you know from your own experience about being in community? One-liners are fine. Does your wisdom make your body happy? Is it doable? Livable? Honest? Share these with someone who affirms you and your life and see how they hold up.

The power of language and belief is that it organizes our thoughts and verbal agreements, and to some extent controls what we can imagine. However, language and belief are never as powerful as action, in my opinion. Future generations learn more from what we embody than what we say. If our words and actions line up, this is integrity. It is one of the greatest gifts we give.

One of my friends has a 15-year-old son who presented a

rolled up scroll to his InterPlaying mom, with a message that recognizes and thanks her for the power in her behaviours.

Mom,
Over the years I've noticed that you're not quite like all the other moms. Most of them are dandy enough, but I can't remember the last time I saw one quite as playful, flamboyant, open, energetic, and nifty as you…and I'm sure none of them can make strange faces quite as well! I thought maybe I'd package this in a unique way to honour your uniqueness.

I'd like to say thank you for both being around, being yourself, and for willing me to go to your concert last evening. Although I admit I wasn't really looking forward to going, I enjoyed myself while there and perhaps more importantly, came to understand you a little better – in a way not possible, perhaps, except at a solo perform-ance. I'm guessing I'll remember last evening long into the future, and appreciate my mother and her dancing belly. Thanks for last night. Thanks for being you. Thanks for everything.

A healthy intellect must be able to include dancing bellies, swing-ing hips, open hearts, and lives flung fully into the arms of play. To think freely, let us trust the structures of the body more and give our minds real range of motion. Let us be honest about what we can and cannot conceive. Let us gladly lean into mys-tery aware of our limitations and receive what we cannot ar-ticulate in words through the languages of movement, stillness, and voice – languages more articulate for research and play in this beautiful, expansive, reality we call life.

———

"A 50-SOMETHING WOMAN AND A 75-YEAR-OLD
GRANDMOTHER WERE BOUNCING OFF ONE ANOTHER LIKE
LITTLE GIGGLY GIRLS."

PAT POTHIER

great grandmother, retired pediatric psychiatric nurse, and
professor, began to dance, find voice, and play in her 70s,
and became a self-pronounced body intellectual.

Lately, I have noticed the pain in my left lower rib area occurs
when my mind is conflicted. I wake up in the morning without
any pain, but the minute I begin to think about something that
is potentially stressful, it sets up enough tension to cause my
ribs to talk to me. "What's happening?" I ask myself. Oh, yeah,
I am undecided about whether to participate in the 5K walk/
run on Sunday.

When I made the decision not to do the race, my body responded to me gently, without pain. Recently, in a support group
at check-in, I talked about my dancing at church as a credit and
my rib pain as a major complaint. Janice asked me if it didn't
hurt to dance. I replied, "My ribs never hurt when I am dancing."

I believe that I have been working on this body/mind connection since I was a little girl. When I was five years old and
suddenly separated from my foster mother, I languished in bed,
ate very little, and would not go out to play. The family doctor
could find nothing wrong with me. Eventually, my bodyspirit
healed enough to let me take up the tasks of growing again.

When I went to live with my mother and sister in my grandmother's house, I started throwing up. I was thrown into an

angry cauldron as my mother and grandmother lived out the unresolved conflicts in their lives and my sister showed her resentment of me in uncomfortable, even dangerous ways. The tension in our house was greatest on weekends, when mother was not working. It was usually on Saturday morning that my body tried to relieve this tension by throwing up at a safe garden spot. When Mom remarried and we moved from that house, the Saturday retching disappeared.

Later, when I was old enough to be a Girl Scout, I saved my money to go to summer camp in the High Sierras. A clean bill of health from a doctor was required to be accepted at camp, so Mom made an appointment with our family doctor. Before we got there I was extremely anxious about the examination. The doctor found me in good health, except for an elevated temperature. Since there didn't seem to be any rationale for the fever, the doctor suggested that we come back in a few days just to take my temperature. When that day came, sure enough I had an elevated temperature again without cause. Without my knowledge, Mom and the doctor conspired. The doctor came to our home unannounced one day and took my temperature and sure enough, I hadn't had time to work it up that day.

I always loved to play in the park just a block from my home. After school, on weekends, and all summer, this park was my second home. I entered the park at a corner by climbing up into the thick bushes, and travelled across the park all the way to the playground without ever touching the ground! I was the Tarzan of Albany Memorial Park! This was real play, completely divorced from any reality of my life except for getting home in time to wash up for dinner. Later in the same park, I learned to shoot baskets and play tennis. However, by this time play had become more mastery than the freedom that comes from just being and using my body for pure fantasy and fun. Of course, with mastery comes the critic. How well am I doing? Am I better than her?

I notice it is hard for me to identify times in my life when I am just having fun. I think I am basically a very serious person. Still, I have enjoyed watching my grandson Dylan (who is now 26 years old) play since he was an infant. Watching grandchildren is a special treat because I don't have to be a parent. I can just watch and indulge. I watched him in his crib playing with the spinning toy that was suspended in front of him. I watched as he learned that his hands and sometimes his feet made the toy spin and make a musical sound. I watched later when he began to crawl and extend his exploring to the larger world. He loved to open cabinet drawers in my kitchen and pull out the pots and pans for nesting and making sound. However, the watching I enjoyed most was when we went to the beach at Santa Cruz, where his father lived. After lathering his red headed fair skin with sunscreen, I would release him to the surf. With his arms wide open, and screaming loudly, he plunged over and over into the waves with great, exuberant abandon.

I miss the feeling of playing with abandon. Most of what I do each day seems to be stuck in the period of mastery and I fear that I have almost lost the pure pleasure of just playing. However, I was reminded that this is still possible for me last Sunday at church. I was standing next to my friend Stacey as we sang Let the Walls Fall Down. We were rocking side to side with the music, and then we began bumping our backsides together and laughing with each bump. Here in the middle of church, a 50-something woman and a 75-year-old grandmother were bouncing off one another like little giggly girls. I want to play with abandon! More play! More fun! More! More! More!

WORDS, VOICE, STILLNESS

LET' EM ALL PLAY

16

BABBLE ON! FREEING YOUR WORDS

Thandiwe Shiphrah of Nashville is a poet. She writes in her book *Leftover Light*,

Have you been happening in this place
without knowing how?
Here, have some light.
Go ahead, feel the heat warming a hole through
the top of your skull.
Breathe in.
And vice versa.
Are you familiar with the concept?
Keep doing it.
Now, think up a word and wave it around in the air.
And there you have it.
Essentially, that's all that's going on here.
Sound
                moving through the centre
                    of a dream.

Imagine an easy body with easy words. What would it be like to let language be a breeze? Surveys show that public speaking is enemy number one, a fate worse than death. Speaking without a script? Impossible.

For me, too, talking was once a bane. I alternated between hating words and trying to possess them. I knew I had things to say, but I didn't know what they were. I was critical of everything I said and how I said it. I avoided speech, drama, and public speaking classes with amazing adeptness. I think I was so afraid of boring or abusing people with words that I almost shut down my ability to speak aloud. When I finally went to seminary and took preaching, I was terrified. I couldn't avoid speaking in public. My overworked sermons came out in tight, punchy spits of truth. A theology paper I wrote began, "Words are like bricks and I am no bricklayer." My mentor and dance colleague, Judith Rock, responded, "Not bricks at all. Words are creatures squirming, flying, leaping, and running around." Dancing words? Words that are free?

My inner urgency to speak wouldn't go away. I wanted the physical freedom of speech that I felt in dance. Oddly, in theatre improvisation I began to find my words even though I was scared every time I had to say something. Gradually, I learned that it didn't matter if I didn't talk in complete sentences or make perfect sense. The adjoining rooms in my brain of self-criticism and language became friendlier neighbours. Practicing babbling, talking freely for short minutes, I lightened up on my way of talking. The split between words and my other ways of knowing healed. Now I rarely use scripts or paper to teach or speak in public. I trust my thinking and my words.

Words are embodied. We tend to think of them as tools of communication instead of being a physical part of who we are. We tend to treat voice, ideas, and words like objects, forgetting that voice, sound, word, breath, and wordlessness is "us." Do you feel blocked when you feel like you don't have a voice – a say in things – or when others tell you they don't want to hear from you? Why? Because you *are* your voice. You *are* your words. Verbal attacks are physical. Words are physicalities. They create physical reaction within us. Being verbal (verb) is to be word in action. Verbal abuse is physical abuse and verbal beauty is physical balm.

Using language in only a focussed, utilitarian way feels heady. Again, our body sense narrows to the small area around our eyes, mouths, and brain as we "think" and talk. We need to remember how to allow words to flow from the bigger body. We need a bigger body bubble for our words.

PRACTICE: THE BODYSPIRIT BUBBLE

Lying on the floor, bring your arms, hands, feet, and legs close to your body. Take a deep breath and for 20 seconds notice how this feels. Next, let your arms and legs fall open with a little more space between your limbs and torso. Breath and notice what this feels like for 20 seconds. Then open your arms and legs all the way out. Notice how this feels. Now place your legs and arms where they feel best to you.

PARTNERED PLAY: BABBLING

Sit with your partner and decide who will go first. Imagine accessing word and voice from your full-body bubble. Instead of trying to force words through the narrow space of your mind like ketchup out of a bottle, imagine sloshing them out. With an easy focus, let your words come as they will. You are not required to be quick, interesting, or amusing. Just talk.

For 30 seconds, let partner one babble about sheep (or any noun that is not too important or meaningful). Next, have partner two babble about laundry. What do you notice? Again, have partner one babble about the sun. Then have partner two babble about farms. Now talk about what you notice together. Shake out your body. Take a deep breath.

For another 30-second exercise, have partner one tell about their backyard. Then, partner two tells about their kitchen.

———

To begin to let words come freely and to trust that they will be there in any moment creates a playful relationship to language. Your words might even become a source of laughter again. As Eva Hoffman said, "Laughter is the lightning rod of play, the eroticism of conversation." This is very difficult for some people and easy for others. In time, each of us is like an author who finds the words to say things that only we can say and only the way we can say them.

Here are some practices you can do alone or with someone else to develop an easier relationship with words.

———

PARTNERED PLAY: BABBLE THIS WAY AND THAT
Remember to use your easy focus and to shake yourself out.
Babble for a minute about your day.
Babble louder.
Babble softer.
Babble from the point of view of a child.
Babble with more silence than words.
Babble about made up things, like besternach or a moochanater.
Babble about a word without using it.
Now just tell about your backyard, kitchen, or a sibling.

———

Babbling about the little details of our lives can lead us back to a love affair with words, especially when we have a willing listener. Listening to someone babble for a minute or two is always interesting. I haven't been bored yet. Knowing that the time is short is part of the magic of staying present. Brevity isn't boring.

Words are magic. It's as if they can come from anywhere. Phil enjoys words so much that when a friend of ours was recovering from illness he spun out this spontaneous, playful prescription in an e-mail to her.

Since you asked for advice, here it is:

Find a chicken that can sing *The Star Spangled Banner*, and whisper your name in its ear three times.

Go to the grocery and touch a green vegetable or two or five and say to yourself, "There's no place like Nome."

Watch reruns of *I Love Lucy* before surgery, but not after.

Draw designs in washable ink on both sides of the scar as a "fashion statement."

On a piece of birch bark (or a yellow sticky if that is easier) draw a circle with a triangle in the middle. Stick that in your left sock on Wednesday for about an hour.

Put a CD in the player upside down and then dance on the ceiling.

After that, feel free to do anything and everything that feels good to you!

XXOO, Phil

We can have a lot more fun with our words. When our words start to babble and flow, rise and fall, jump and gallop again, a fire ignites in us and our words can heal. Truth comes more easily. Brian Herring's poem *Fire in the Mouth* beautifully illuminates this.

I am a man with a fire in my mouth
I am a man whose stories have not been told
I am a man who believed
that I had no stories of my own
and if I did
who would listen?

My stories lie piled
around my feet
like the leaves of an old tree
they have become dry and brittle.

But a spark has struck them
a spark of light
a spark of Life
they are transformed
into something new
and bright
there is a wildfire on my tongue.

Tongues of Fire,
lick over me
wash my wounds.

———

"I FOUND WAYS TO SHARE THE HEART
OF WHAT I KNOW."

BOB KAPLAN,

a spiritual counsellor, found it easier and more powerful
to communicate about spirit when he could use both his words
and movement.

If a picture is worth a thousand words, then how many words is a dance worth? I had never contemplated that question until I found myself telling my stories through dance and movement. I was at an InterPlay workshop, rediscovering my body's inherent wisdom and having lots of fun. One afternoon we were invited to try something called dance/talk. In dance/talk, an individual goes out on the dance floor and alternates dancing with talking. Something inside moved me to the dance floor, even though I had never even seen a demonstration of dance/talk, nor had any idea how I would dance or what I would talk about.

So despite my reservations I started dancing. Toward the end of my first short dance, I found myself moving toward my audience. It was time for me to talk, but I didn't have a clue what I wanted to say. I didn't even have a theme in mind! I danced myself to within a few feet of my audience, looked up at them, and then noticed the interesting position my arms had taken. Out came a short story about a hike I had taken that morning!

Once again I took off across the floor dancing improvisationally. And once again my body led me into telling a totally improvisational story. This time I became a conductor with the audience as my pretend musicians. By the time I did my third dance/talk, I had the audience laughing and thoroughly engaged. I had discovered something very powerful and magical within me. I had discovered my performer!

The next day we were invited to try again, with a new twist. This time I combined dancing and talking into one continuous flow. And this time I performed with a theme in mind. I still didn't know how I would dance, nor what I would say. I just knew that I would let it all flow as naturally and as spontaneously as the previous day. The only difference was that I knew that I would share movements and stories inspired by my years of communicating with spirit realm.

I went out to the dance floor and let my body guide me. Within a minute I was sharing stories and insights and subtle concepts that normally take me days to write about. With a few moves and a few words, I showed how I had learned to step across the veils which seemingly separate human beings from spirit beings. And with a very simple gesture, I demonstrated the essence of my work which is to help people to reconnect with their deceased loved ones and to discover that their love never ends. I had spent months creating a website about this work and these ideas. But in minutes of combining dancing with storytelling, I found ways to share the heart of what I know. Wow!

In recent years, I've been doing some dance, especially authentic movement. And I've been doing a lot of improvisational theatre and some storytelling as part of the Living Story Theatre Group. But it had never occurred to me to put them all together until I was at that InterPlay workshop. My bodywisdom drew them all together and showed me the magic that exists within me as an improvisational performer/storyteller/dancer.

Now when I contemplate problems or next steps in my life, I know to consult my bodywisdom. Sometimes it's a matter of going inside and finding new guidance. And sometimes I need to get up, move around, do a little dance, and allow my body's natural movements to show new answers. So now I spend less time thinking out solutions and more time opening to my body and allowing my innate creativity and bodywisdom to lead me to new solutions.

A great example of this happened while I was writing this story. I set an intention for myself to be more openhearted. Generally, I can keep such intentions in my mind for only seconds before other thoughts and feelings intrude, then I bring my mind back to my intention, forget it, remember it, etc. I took this intention to my authentic movement group and did a 20-minute dance of open heartedness. For my mind, 20 minutes of open heartedness is an eternity, but for my body it was easy. I kept my focus on my heart for the entire 20-minute dance, and I felt blissed out for days afterward. My bodywisdom leads me to body bliss.

17

VOCAL BODIES

The first time I heard Trisha Watts sing, something in me felt heard. She dreams through a voice as big as the world. This world voice is in many of us. It is intimate and powerful. As a prophet of song, she knows that when our voice becomes embodied, we are free. She asks:

What would it be to step into our musical bloodstreams and invite a radical trust in the Voice that flows within in us all?

What would it be to sing up soul grounded in a contemporary community that dares to anchor in play, mischievousness, and profound honesty?

To stand on the shoulders of our cultural ancestors and chant out incantations with the choirs of angels that surround us?

What would it be to join hands, hearts, and voices with our sisters and brothers from around the world, in a body of sound that is a living harmony and a witness of solidarity and a communion of belonging?

Would it be madness? Certainly.

Would it be a cacophony? Indeed.

Could it be a living peace? YES!

It is exactly this kind of dreaming and imagination that I practice in my life and commitment with the InterPlay community in Australia and overseas.

Singing is the greatest joy and animator of spirit I know. To animate is to invoke, awaken, and call up soul. We have as a community, as a body of wisdom, an opportunity to be a voice of compassion and hope in a very disturbed yet regenerative world.

To sing alone, solo, has its own unique beauty and place, but to sing together unashamedly with an intent of freedom, justice, and reconciliation, creates an energy and vibration that moves mountains and organically grows new landscapes for dialogue and dwelling.

Stepping into this fullness note by note, and trusting in a Voice that goes deeper, higher, and wider than our own single bodies, connects us with a presence, a mystery, that reminds us we are more than flesh and bone; we are singing creatures, eternal and deeply loved.

The great play of the voice can lift the world from depression, but what if we are still afraid of making the wrong sound in public? How do we unlock and have our voices?

I was using a large noisy machine to sand away layers of gunk on the floor of our building. Every part of me and the room shook. T-Bone, the dry-wall man, was taping and topping nearby. Every now and then I would stop, take a deep breath, and spontaneously release a long, loud sigh.

"You okay?" he asked.

"Sure," I laughed. "That's just what I do to let go of tension. You should try it!" Pretty soon he was doing it, too.

"Hey, that feels good," he said.

The two of us intermittently cracked up as we worked and sighed. We were playing. No wonder people used to sing group work songs. Breathing, vocalizing, and moving together makes labour easier.

———

PRACTICE: A DEEP BREATH AND A SIGH

Take a deep breath and let it out with a big, long sigh. Do it again. Let all the breath go out of you. Take a deep breath and let the sigh be as loud as you can. Feel the vibrations from the sigh. This is like massage on the inside.

————

A sigh gives voice to life. Sounds reveal scores about us: our emotions, our energy, our wild inner story, the call of our imagination. Even silence is full of the sacred potency of sound. The first letter of the ancient Hebrew alphabet, *aleph*, anticipates the split second before sound: potential voice. The Hebrew word *ruah* means spirit and breath. That pressure in the throat, the ache in the chest, the lyric pushing up from within, dancing in the back of our head – that breath is our vocal potential.

Yet it's odd to make noise out loud. From early childhood we are told over and over, "Be quiet! Be quiet! Be quiet!" Why? Because we are so incredibly and constantly vocal. Learning to be quiet is a good thing. However, it would be even better if we were also shown when and how to have our full voice. Unfortunately, we just keep putting away our voice bit by bit until all we have left is a voice box. When we no longer experience our voices filling our own bodies, much less a room, we shut off the body wisdom that can only come through vocalizing.

We take the voice far, far too seriously. To start with, we need to let go of trying to have a good voice. The voice is wild. It is emotional and weird and an incredibly fun inventor.

————

MEDITATION: "VOCAL PLAY,"
LIKE BREATHING, #10–13

These improvisations reveal the crazy fullness, rhythm, and fun of voices at play. With titles like "Fried Chicken," "Play," "Freedom," and "Release," our voices go wild. Laugh with us. If our voices are to be our muse, let them amuse.

———

To let voice spill forth is an adventure. Start with curiosity, affirmation, and fun, and go from there.

PLAY: TEN-SECOND FAKE SONGS

For ten seconds each, sing fake opera, fake country western, jazz or blues, gospel, rock, or whatever else feels easy, silly, and fun. If it's hard, know that it's often easier to play with others than alone. In the spirit of faking it, let go of singing right. Sing a secret lullaby to someone you love that can begin with the still small voice within, our inside voice.

———

We have been taught to use our voice. As adults and as children, having our voice for ourselves is just as important. If valuable information comes through our voice, information that can come in any other way, then we need time to allow our voice to move, and breathe, and have its being. We need to hear what we have to say, sing, and sound like to ourselves. Taking the voice out of the lime light and bringing into a sheltered place can help.

———

PLAY: THE STILL, SMALL VOICE

Cup your hands around your mouth to form a container for your inside voice. Take a deep breath, then, as you exhale, engage your vocal chords just slightly. Let your voice come into the small space you have created with your hands. As you continue to exhale, let your voice move gently into this small space.

PLAY: TAKE A VOCAL JOURNEY

Now, inside the intimate space of your cupped hands, take a deep breath and let your voice wander higher, lower, and around. Once you get going, it may surprise you that your voice can come so easily. Take another breath. If words come, fine. If not, that's fine too. This vocal play is only for you. You are listening to your own voice and having your voice for yourself.

———

The ability to hear and match the sounds of others does not determine your ability to sing. Vocal power resides in physical commitment to your own voice. Over and over I witness singers come forth who had no clue that their voices were treasures. They had judged themselves based on external rules about singing. It was difficult or impossible to imagine that they could start just with the voice that was there. Many had been told, "Don't sing," and who doesn't compare themselves to outstanding vocalists. Why even open our mouths? We concede vocal fullness to the priests of voice: rock and rollers, operatic princes, ranters and ravers of the stage. We may only feel free in a huge stadium to sing and dance along, or sometimes in the privacy of the shower or car.

The point of having our voices is to have ourselves: to enjoy, know, and hear ourselves, and to move energy in our gut and heart. Voice vibrates and dances us from inside out: rattling, baying, yelling, whispering, cooing, snorting, humming, sobbing, serenading, chanting. We can let the sound flow from us in every act of pain and glee.

It is critical to have your own voice. Spiritual teachers around the world warn that those who lose their song, lose their soul. Be it lullaby, freedom song, lament, or war cry, the body's song keeps us alive in the most difficult circumstances.

PLAY: ONE-BREATH-AT-A-TIME SINGING

Lying or sitting, take a deep breath and let it out with one long sigh. Use all the breath you have. On your next deep breath, move your mouth and face as you release the tone. Notice how this affects your sound. On another out-breath, let your voice squirm around in your head from high to low. Now let your voice go where it wants, making a one-breath song. Keep adding one breath as you enjoy following your sounds.

My deepest prayers come through my voice. Vocalizing physically integrates my images and feelings. Like the Psalms (the songs in the Hebrew Bible), Mary's sigh "too deep for words," Jesus' cry at the death of his friend Lazarus, or chants to Allah, nothing else moves us like vocal music. It is emotional. No wonder religious and cultural piety has its deep anchoring in song. Listen to people around the world whose sounds come in every modality, dynamic, and texture. It is all there. It is all ours. Take it. Sing your song right now. Sing on behalf of someone you love. Sing for the world. Be like Oliver Crichton whose poetry sings what his body wants.

I want to be a wide-mouth jar,
container of wisdom and spiller at the same time.
I want to be a jar that feels full, not empty.
I want to be a jar that sings.

"WHAT JOY TO FIND SPACE TO EXPAND
OR JUST TO SING A SONG IN PEACE
AND NON-JUDGMENT."

JONATHAN LEAVY

Jonathan Leavy's career in musical theatre almost cost him his
innate joy in life.

Performing was my life. I could not get enough of it all, the
make-up, the applause, the stories brought to life, and mostly
the magic of the theatre. That indescribable energy that exists
between the people on stage and the people in the audience
became my lifeblood.

My first performing job was not a small one; I went big! I
spent my first summer out of high school dancing in the pa-
rades at Walt Disney World, earning money doing what I loved
to do! Near the end of college I landed my first professional
theatre job, acting in an authentic Victorian melodrama in Cripple Creek, Colorado. And in a company of ten, doing 12 shows
a week with one day off, I was happy. I learned the art of mo-
notony, as I like to call it, making each of those 161 shows that
summer look like the first time.

I finished college and BOOM! went right to New York City
to audition. I did well, landing jobs that took me to Roanoke,
Virginia, and a national touring show which performed in high
schools. Moving to Florida, I accepted roles in a dinner theatre
production, as a dancing sea turtle at Sea World, and was hired
by Disney to sing in the Hoop-Dee-Doo Revue and to be a street
actor in the United Kingdom pavilion. When the Disney performers chose to join the union, I got my Actors' Equity card,
which allowed me to perform in union houses with bigger budg-
ets and (supposedly) higher quality productions.

Life as an Equity Actor was very different. I needed to go where the work was. I spent less time at home in Orlando and more time out on the road. And an odd thing started to happen. Some jobs I took were enjoyable and challenging, but others felt like a lot of hard work and were less fun.

Around that time I was chosen to replace the Phantom in a running production of *Phantom* in Sarasota, Florida. This was a dream come true for me. My name was above the title in a successful production in which I was the lead. I named my own salary and the show ran a long time. This was the peak of my professional career and I was able to sign with a talent manager, moved back to New York City, and got my own apartment.

After ten years of performing, I grew weary of the cycles – audition a lot, get no work, audition a lot more, get a job, have fun, go back to auditioning, get no work, audition a lot more, etc. That is when I hit my all-time low. With loneliness, a cold winter, and the end of a long-term relationship, I was depressed. I had lost my joy. I began therapy.

Over time, I shifted more and more energy to my spiritual life in prayer, meditation, and journalling. I attended the church of my choice, as opposed to the church that would hire me to sing. The associate pastor had also spent years of his life performing. I really enjoyed discussing theatre and spirituality with him. I became a regular at his weekly spirit group for artists. What a fascinating time it was to witness other artists who were concerned about the same things, such as, "How do I keep my creativity flowing while also earning a living in this city?"

It became clear to me that I did not want to live in NYC any more. My spirit was dying. It was very hard for me to acknowledge that feeling because it conflicted with my goal of performing on Broadway. Then, as if from heaven, I got a phone call telling me that I had been hired to sing and dance on a cruise ship in Alaska! I took the job and spent that summer not only out of the big city, but out of my worries.

My spirit and body loved living on water and seeing huge mountains all around, eagles flying overhead, and whales showing up at the most beautiful moments! There were days when I would just sit on the open deck and breathe deeply for an hour or more. I made a routine out of starting each day with a candle and silence, waking up early to watch the glaciers calve into the sea. I also watched the daily sunsets. I was finding peace.

I performed on board three days a week. Eventually, I volunteered to lead worship services for passengers, which became more rewarding and fulfilling than doing the shows. The next summer I returned to the ship and stayed on board until January. During that time I dropped my manager in New York and discovered much more of who I was as a person, as a creation. Broadway was thousands of miles away and I was the happiest I had ever been!

Surprisingly, even to me, I applied and was accepted to a seminary with a focus on the arts: Pacific School of Religion in Berkeley, California. When I got off the ship, I had a new direction. I was amazed to be surrounded by artists, people of varying faiths and different sexual orientations, all in one community learning about theology and each other. However, I had to make adjustments in my patterns: how to sit in a classroom, take notes, study, and write papers. Harder still, I had to adjust to not being on stage. It was odd to let a week, then a month go by without having an audience. After several months I began to settle into myself, into my body, and into this new and different lifestyle.

I thank the Divine guidance I received when I chose to take Cynthia Winton-Henry's InterPlay class my first semester. Here was a spiritually-focussed class, using bodies and voices to reconnect with others and ourselves. Slowly, I began to discover that singing and dancing do not always have to be done for others. I found how my body could heal from the high expectations I placed on it. I began to remember how much I loved to dance around the room, sing in a circle, and just be silly. Who knew that I would have to come to a seminary across the county to find the Jonathan who just loved to sing and dance as he did in his living room!?

I used this playful way of being through all three years of my master's program. I would breathe deeply, sighing audibly in classes at times, shake my body out while writing papers, and sing sing sing in my apartment, at chapel services, and even while walking across campus. I was doing it all for me! Instead of dropping my gifts of song and dance, I began incorporating them into my everyday life. Teaching voice lessons, dancing in church services, and leading workshops, I made play a serious part of my life.

The hardest area for me was to play with my public singing. Letting go of the "right and wrong" ways of singing (how to stand, breathe, emote, project, etc.) took a long time. I loosened up my body, moved more while I sang, and with practice began to feel more and more comfortable singing improvisationally, trusting the creative inspiration of the moment.

Today I am happy. I am a Minister of the Arts. My understanding of the Divine is still very personal, but now, standing in front of people to create a song/dance/story is one the holiest of times for me. I have come to know that I am called to help others in this area of the voice, to show how our voices are part of our bodies and spirits, hearts and minds. In vocal sessions with people, I focus on each person's voice and how it is embodied. I delight in working with non-singers, people who have been told they couldn't or shouldn't sing. Deeply thirsting for vocal release, vocal freedom, and vocal community, we find space to expand or just sing a song in peace and non-judgment. This is my ministry, my return to the dance of life.

18

STILLNESS IS OUR FRIEND

Stillness is not an absence of movement. For those who move about on this planet, it is the heart of the dance, central to the whole dance of life and change. T. S. Eliot, in "Four Quartets," reminds us that "except for the point – the stillpoint, there would be no dance and there is only the dance."

In Thailand, I visited the temple of the great reclining golden Buddha. Leaving my shoes at the door and entering the immense room, I found it completely filled with a beatific being, two stories high, skin shimmering like the sun. Buddha lay as still as water. His faint smile, mouth effortlessly turned up at the corners, eyes open but easy, as though they could either open or close – everything in his expression was poised in grace. Overwhelmed by such beauty and ease, I was newly encouraged that somewhere in the world our highest self is at rest. After so many years of dwelling on images of God suffering on the cross, or leading people on perilous journeys to escape persecution, this contemplation of divinity rooted in stillness and easy peace was radical. The body wants the dance of peace.

"Sit still!" are words graffitied on the early memory of every child I know. No wonder. Holding still is not our native way. Children are movers. Squirming is easier than holding still. Most of us have to learn to settle down. We gradually get the idea that stillness is different than moving. This is an unfortunate split for many of us, one that makes peace harder to claim. We resist sitting and feel restless. To regain the quiet at the centre of our own whirlwinds, InterPlayers laugh and practice sneaking up on stillness, saying, "Stillness is our friend."

PRACTICE: EASE UP ON HOLDING STILL

Hold perfectly still for 30 seconds. What do you notice? Now take a deep breath and shake yourself out a little. For a little while, simply have the stillness that is there. What do you notice?

Holding still can cause muscles to tighten and breath to go shallow. Instead of quieting, we can grow more tense. This stillness is too hard and we know it. Real stillness is alive like a butterfly in us, its wings moving gently, imperceptibly. The common picture associated with being still may look like going within and getting small. This is only a picture.

PLAY: FILL'ER UP WHEN STILLNESS COMES

Instead of contracting your bodyspirit, expand it. Open your arms so that you can feel your width. Raise your arms overhead so that you can feel how tall and vertically connected you are to heaven and earth. Dance or go outside. Don't resist your energy. Let yourself move. Soon you will come to a place that feels and is still. Hang out there as long as you like. Two minutes can be a blessed eternity when you enter the dancing stillness.

Stillness is required in life more than we might like. Standing and sitting in lines, in meetings, in cars, and at desks, we may feel confined, restless, edgy, stuck, and wish we were doing something, anything else. Gravity's burden on muscles and bones, especially the spine, lessens if we remain in movement. Standing easy allows our bodyspirit to move in stillness. You can dance anywhere you are asked to be still, if you can stand easy.

PRACTICE: EASY KNEES BODY

Stand and take a deep breath. Rather than lock your legs and spine, soften your knees and let your weight shift around on the soles of your feet. Imagine being in a redwood grove. Tilt your head back and look up through the branches. Like a tree, you can be rooted and still without being stiff. Bring your focus back down to earth. Stand easy.

Silence and stillness are active states, power postures that align our bodyspirits with the dance of life. Instead of being polar opposites, movement and rest are woven together in the improvisation of living. The movement of breath is also central to stillness.

PRACTICE: ROCK INTO STILLNESS

Take some deep breaths. Let them out with a sigh. Simultaneously rock or sway. Enjoy breathing as you rock. As your rocking grows smaller and smaller, hang out inside this little dance.

In the artful dance of life, our freedom to move into and out of stillness is a great gift. The law of inertia recognizes that a body in motion remains in motion and a body at rest remains at rest. Once we start moving, we keep moving. Fortunately, humans are not rocks tumbling to the bottom of a hill to rest there for an eon. We are moment-to-moment creators responding to the ongoing play of energy and matter. We can stop and start with the phrasing and grace of a dancer. We do not have to fight inertia. Be hospitable. Welcome stillness. Indulge it when it comes. This nourishes soul. Dancing in stillness we make contact with our inner sabbath.

PLAY: DANCE, SHAPE, STILLNESS, AND BREATH:
"BODY PRAYER," *LIKE BREATHING*, #1

Place a hand in the air. Notice its shape. Make a new shape with your hand. Notice what it is like to be in this shape. Breathe and flow into new shapes. Now quickly change from shape to shape with each stillness. Notice what it is like to place your hand intentionally in a shape. Try making some weird shapes. Begin a dance of shape, stillness, breath, and change. Notice when you just want quiet. Sink into and rise out of stillness as desired. When your dance is over, notice if a sense of stillness comes with completion.

———

In stillness we come home not to lack of movement or life, but to the simplest movement of all – just standing, sitting, or lying there breathing. Stillness is the ground that offers the well and the springboard for holy play. Stillness lets us notice that we have arrived, one body and soul. Beverly Voss' poem BodySpirit calls us to this place of unity, and to what the body wants.

I want my spirit
to be a gentleness
that says to body:
There, there!

It's quite all right.
It's quite all right.
I want my body
to sigh the world's deepest sigh
and hear those words (those ancient words):
All is well
and all is well
and all manner of thing shall be well.
I want spirit to burrow into marrow and blood.
To flow on red rivers
that course through
liver and spleen.
I want body to hear spirit's hum
as she rides the waves that
breath and lungs create.
I want body and spirit to move as one.
For spirit to shiver
when hand up-scoops
winter snow.
For body to shake when spirit laughs.
For spirit to rest when body says Done!
For them to weave/flow/
sing/sleep/weep/
stomp/laugh and cavort.
To tell tall tales and small truths.
To find the mulberry tree
to climb.
The poem to dance.
The song to chant.
The lips to kiss.
The fire to light.

———

"I JUST COULD NOT BE STILL."

CYNTHIA WINTON-HENRY

I consider my reunion with stillness one of my greatest accomplishments. A friend once joked I might have "attention intensity disorder." I had so much energy that to sit still was either painful, or I fell asleep. People spoke of the virtues of quiet contemplation. Stillness should be a basic human ability, yet I did not possess it. I was rest-less. Something in my body perpetually resisted quiet. Was I addicted to my adrenalin, keeping a steady flow of it running to prevent something bad from rising up? I pretended to be happy. But peaceful? Peace seemed a myth. Thank God I slept well. When I put my head down, out I went. Otherwise, I doubt I could have functioned for as long as I did.

Family and friends were constantly concerned. "Was I getting enough downtime? Time off? How are you?" they'd ask. "You seem tired." When I was pastoring a church in Sunnyvale, California, I counted work hours obsessively to make sure I wasn't over-working. What could I do?

It helped to learn that my kinesthetic make-up was rooted in thrusting, being on the go. Just like my dad who is in his 70s and runs 100-mile mountain races, activity gave me the physical sensation of grace. The energy in my body had to go somewhere. Sitting around filled me with tension. Consequently, I've accomplished a tremendous amount. But at home, plunking down on the couch, all I had left for loved ones was irritability. My husband regularly expressed frustration at me, wishing I could settle down.

Meanwhile, Phil implored Wing it! – our improvisational

performance company – to use more stillness. "It's easy to move," he'd say. "You already know how to do that. I want stillness!" We were terrible at it and I was the most rebellious of all. Even when I thought I was still, he'd tell me I'd barely stopped. "Ninety percent stillness this time!" he'd say, and we'd all go cross-eyed and joke, "Stillness is our friend." But gradually, we got better at it.

One month before my 41st birthday, I hit that notorious midlife speed bump. My metabolic clock ratcheted down – kathunk. "Uh-oh," I heard myself say. I knew I was in trouble. Nothing would ever be the same. My body suddenly slowed, but I didn't know how to go with it. I began to experience energy droughts. Depression snuck in, intensifying my imaginative inner life. One year later on Friday the 13th, Good Friday, after picking up my income tax bill, I broke down. Feeling bankrupt and in debt at so many levels, thighs aching, unstoppable tears, so tired that every action was an effort, a dark hole in my chest yawned open. All I could do was rest, but it was still hard. Medication helped. Months of recuperation helped. But anytime I was told to hold still a quivery, high-pitched frequency raged inside me.

Phyllis, a long-time friend and guide knew my difficulty. One day she took the bull by the horns. In a meditation group she announced, "Today we're getting to the bottom of this, Cynthia. Bring your chair to the centre of the circle." Phyllis guided my imagination toward the source of my unrest. Descending through a series of images, with deep breaths, I finally came upon what I most dreaded. I saw myself as a young child pinned down by a large adult male. Terrified, I felt rage communicating back over the decades. My body hated being held still.

Many of my dreams, sensations, and intuitions now made sense. I released that memory. But remembering the trauma was only part of the dilemma. As we say in InterPlay, to change my life I would still have to change my practice.

One day, I asked my friend Steve Harms about stillness. He is a Lutheran minister able to be content for weeks in the silence of a Trappist monastery. He shrugged as if he hadn't a clue, laughed like he always does, and then quoted T. S. Eliot: "In stillness, moving still." My eyes widened. In that instant I knew how deeply I had internalized the belief that stillness is the opposite of moving. With T. S. Eliot's little koan in my heart, I began moving backwards into stillness as if sneaking up on it. Dancing improvisationally, I discovered I actually did have moments of peace and quiet as my thoughts, emotions, and desires moved and cleared away. Over time, these moments lengthened. A spacious simplicity unfolded in me as the miracle of effortless tranquility became mine again.

Now, I love my solitude, the well of peace. There is nothing to keep me from it except the ordinary challenges of a crazy 21st-century life. It is enough to be.

I put my foot down
bent over
eyes counting
step step step
still.

I stand up
hand on my heart
look ahead
close my eyes.
still.

I see those
I carried,
now dancing
on their own
still.

Grateful my feet
on the earth
the sun
each morning
finally
still.

ECSTATIC COMMUNITY
THE GROUP BODY

19

CONTAGIOUS COMMUNITY HEALTH

I noticed it first when I was in youth choir. We would be singing and I would get this wonderful feeling. I felt more open and electrically charged. I realized it must have to do with the group body singing all together. At the time, I wondered if this feeling was what people called God. Later, I felt it in dancing with others, particularly when the intent of the dance was spiritually based. I knew these experiences as communion. Teaching improvisationally, I have often felt moments of great unity with groups, able to draw on a wisdom greater than my own. Ecstatic community has been a consistent part of my experience just as communities of tension and disharmony are part of me.

The group is within each one of us. When a crowd stands, we are pulled to standing. At the office, we sense when something is going on. At accidents or fires, our bodies slow down, sensing trouble. I sense my family, the body of my nation, and sometimes the entire earth in my own body. When my nation suffers, I suffer. We are not independent cogs. The well-being of the group is our own well-being.

A body kinesthetically identifies with the movement of a whole group. If I come to work feeling great, my work group can still drain me. Even if my community is far away, I carry deep body memories of them. There is a "we" in me. Because many of us are not conditioned to think of ourselves as a group body unless we are on a sports team or are physically performing together, we may not notice the physical experience of community in our own body or know how to talk about it.

Human groups are earth organisms, physical, of the earth. Traces of this truth lie in our language. "Corporate" springs from corpus, meaning body. Incarnate comes from "in the flesh." "Organization" implies organs. The health of the tribe or group is a primal concern. Designed as communal creatures, we huddle, cluster, eat, sleep, and create together. We are one with our group, even when the group is broken or unsatisfying.

JOURNAL: PICTURE YOUR GROUP BODY

Consider your family or work group as a body of people. On the whole, are they energetic? Playful? Spiritual? Do they take a lot of space or a little? What kind of animal would they be? Are they forward-moving or reluctant? Active or passive? Industrious, busy, quiet, scattered, focussed? In your torso (heart, solar plexus, belly, groin) do you notice physical sensations when you remember them. Are the connections strong, weak, warm, cool, non-existent? Sometimes they only become noticeable when we move away. Home-sickness is a malaise of the body for our familiar place and group.

We may minimize our profound body-to-body connection, but we cannot get out of it. We are physically connected, perhaps even after we die.

To be able to create the physicality of grace in our communities, particularly in an individualistic culture, requires that we intentionally remember that each individual carries the group body within themselves. We simultaneously maintain our wonderful individuality and nourish the communal body when we learn that individual and community are not opposites, but dance together within us all. Our bodies are both individual and communal physicalities.

We walk. We stop. We run in patterns and at tempos that unite us. Thirty-five miles per hour. Left turn only. Please be seated. Line forms here. The architecture of society affects our movement. We feel independent as we concentrate on our own paths, but we are dancing together, accelerating, slowing down, and matching each other more than we can acknowledge.

If you want more joy and creativity in community, the simple play of walking, stopping, and running is a tonic. Don't settle for unconsciously letting your environments control your dance. Play an active role in the dance of group life. In fact, embodied play is the multi-vitamin of communal health. A group that plays together often stays together.

PARTNERED PLAY: WALK, STOP, AND RUN: "STRUT AND JIVE,"
LIKE BREATHING, #6

Get three or more people in a space where there is room to move. Walk in any direction without talking. Change direction. Find the edges of your space as well as the centre. Walk slowly. Walk fast. Walk backwards. If you run into someone, say "thank you" instead of "I'm sorry." Walk in an unpredictable path. Run if you are able. Run right by something/someone. Walk in step with somebody. Walk on your own. Stop and enjoy stillness. Now play with walking, stopping, running, and each other on your own time. You can do this in silence or with the _Like Breathing_ music playing. "Strut and Jive" carries the easy-going spirit of this dance. When you finish, share what you notice. In InterPlay, we walk stop and run together like this often. It is free and open and allows individual bodies to relate without over conformity. It's a kind of folk dance for the 21st century.

―――

My friend Randy secretly played walking, stopping, and running, with strangers on the beach. He found connections and access to the greater dance of life even though he was the only one aware of it. His willingness to play in the world this way makes him one of the happier, more mystical, and more amused people I know.

The dance of walking, stopping, and running is not a rule-driven dance. By tuning up the group sense, each person can participate from a place of choice. Many possibilities occur. All seem relevant – moving on one's own, being swept into someone else's movement, tricking, flirting, leaning, standing still with others. Given freedom and permission, people easily move toward both individual and communal fullness. As we trust our body's creative instincts, we can experience the joyful possibilities within community. Oddly, we are being fully ourselves, yet a group connection forms like no other. Physical camaraderie enables participants to experience a group in unity.

A thriving group consists of thriving individuals. The more we can claim our individual physical style, energy, and truth, the more fullness and fun the group can have. Kinesthetic presence affects the whole. Consider your family. Each family member's body communicates deeper than words. A good parent knows that his or her greatest legacy is in actions that move directly to their children. Love, joy, beauty, and life leap directly from body to body.

The group body wants play, creative challenge, rest, and communion. The body does not want to suffer. Dreams, visions, religion, education, and the body politic are born from our desire for grace. We are here not just to put an end to suffering, but to have true grace. Many traditions believe that our actions (and therefore our bodies) have an effect on seven generations to come. Each body in community has the potential to change history for better and for worse. Since health is contagious, then bodies that move freely, breathe deeply, and play fully can change the world for the better. This is love. Avatar Meher Baba says, "Those who do not have it catch it from those who have it. True love is unconquerable and irresistible, and it goes on gathering itself until eventually it transforms everyone whom it touches." When this occurs, well-being spreads through the crowd faster than anyone imagined it would. A playful ethic emerges as bodies surrender, struggle, and bless what they have. I know because I have seen it again and again on stage, backstage, in classes, at retreats, in prisons, and in the lives of so many unlikely dancers. After witnessing an astonishing diversity of people in an InterPlay performance called *The Unbelievable Beauty of Being Human,* my joy and awe burst into poetry. Susanne Mulcahy, turned this poem into a song.

MEDITATION: "PICTURE THIS,"
LIKE BREATHING, #19

Listen to "Picture This." Imagine you are in someone's living room at a house concert where playful folks are singing and being themselves in community. It's a simple thing, and magnificent.

Picture this!
People not afraid to touch.
Children looking up
to dancing elders.
Rowdy lovers, every one
snatched up in each other's arms.
Hips curved,
hair clipped or flying,
opposites attracting,

stories of consequence,
failure, curse,
trust and victory.

Picture this!
A southern white millionaires
and a black man embrace.
An ex-con and suburbanite dancing.
Addicts full of only themselves.
Pagan and Christian laughing.
A lesbian mom taking centre stage.
Gay and straight men carry on
and everyone is in love with the beauty
of an unwed mom!

Picture thousands of stages,
altars, halls, and schools
as home to dancing bodies.
Hospital workers singing to those in bed.
Song and dance raised up in prison,
ghetto, and war zone.
Fear taking second place to love
as we know we are
each other's daily bread.

I have seen all this again and again
in the gathering of willing players.
Unbelievably beautiful
so believably human.
Can you picture this?

———

"BROTHERS AND SISTERS, IS THERE
SOMETHING HOLDING YOU BACK FROM
A DANCE YOU YEARN TO DANCE?"

BRENT BISETTE

a gay man called to ministry, did more than preach about his
longing for embodied, accepting, life and love in community – he
danced it. This is his sermon, "Dancing is Dangerous."

My life-partner, Rich, and I attended a wedding recently. All in
all it was a lovely wedding. Oh, it had its share of sexism and
fluff, as most weddings do. But the bride and groom were mid-
life and entering second marriages. They had a certain amount
of chutzpah that told you they were about more than following roles; they were going to get down to the nitty-gritty together, given half a chance. After the wedding, there was a lively
reception at the Holiday Inn. And after the perfunctory intro-
ductions, a four-course meal.

We got to my favourite part of the reception, the dancing.
Well, sort of. There is always the dilemma. Do we or don't we?
I looked at Rich and he looked at me as if to say, Shall we dance?
I'd love to, but do we know these people well enough to take
the chance? They belong to kind of a conservative church. Will
anyone make a scene? I'd hate to ruin the bride and groom's
wedding. And, if it became necessary, I don't run well in these
tight dress shoes. All this communication was going on, you
understand, without speaking. We've had this conversation
before, many times. I calmly squeezed Rich's hand under the
table cloth, as if to say, "It's okay, you know I love you, and
that's what matters," while inside my gut was doing somer-

saults. It's not fair! They get to share their love without a thought. They get to dance with their honey and celebrate their most intimate relationship while I get to sit here and smile and play with my fork. Ahhhh!

It has slowly and painfully occurred to me over the past seven years since I came out as a gay man that my righteous anger has left me feeling lonely and depressed more days than I care to tell you. It has occurred to me that I am holding on to my anger at my culture and especially at my church. Anger which I believe to be entirely righteous has left me closer to bitter chains than to freedom.

I have wept over the church of Jesus Christ and its sins. I have selfishly wept over the loss of my status as a privileged, white, heterosexual male. I have wept over the loss of the vocational path to ministry that I felt called to again and again. And I have stewed with anger. But I confess to you that something is changing in my body and in my soul.

(At this point in the sermon, the InterPlay community dances together in the front of the sanctuary playing with walking, stopping, and running.)

My brothers and sisters, is there something holding you back from a dance you yearn to dance? Are you on the inside looking out? Or the outside looking in? Either way, are you missing connection to the people whom you want to touch and be touched by? What is it that grabs your righteous anger? Are you limited by cultural prejudice? Or emotional hurt? Or physical challenge?

I don't blame you for being angry. It's part of our gloriously God-given humanness, but I'd advise you not to hold on to it. At least, that's what I'm learning for myself. Have it and then let go. Don't let your anger and resentment keep you from the dance. Let your anger dance so you can too.

If you cannot dance with the church, then dance in the streets. If you cannot dance with the Republican Party or the Democratic Party, then dance with the disenfranchised. If you cannot stand on your own feet to dance, then shout and wave your hands. But for God's sake and for the sake of a world that needs your unique gifts, find a way to dance! Yes, I know, there are days when I want to dance but, given my circumstances, don't know how. There are days, many days, when I need help. And on those days especially, dance your dance of sorrow and helplessness and yearning, but try to dance it where someone can see you – anyone, especially God. Because whatever the tempo of your dance, mournful and slow, erratic and changing, steady and joyful, someone else is dancing it, too.

And when you dance together you find community, and you challenge the powers that threaten your dance of life. For we are created by a God who calls us to dance. We serve a Christ who leads us in the dance. We are empowered by a Spirit who dances within and around us, healing our hurts and limitations, which would seek to hold us back, and celebrating our unique rhythm.

But I must also warn you! Dancing is dangerous. It is not only dangerous because we can use passion for evil, it is dangerous because when the music begins and you take the dance floor, you lose control of who might join you in the dance – gay or straight or bisexual or transgendered; black or white or Latino or Asian; man or woman; walking or riding a wheelchair; conservative or liberal; insider or outsider. And you lose control of where the music might lead you together, if you truly open wide the dance of your life.

But the alternative, as I have discovered it, is to sit alone holding on to your anger or your hurt, looking out a window at the dance, like David's wife who looked down at David dancing in the courtyard below.

The Lord of the Dance came for life abundant. The Lord of the Dance invites us out of isolation and into community. Come join the dance, with all your heart and body and soul and strength! Come and give yourself to the scary, exhilarating, mystifying dance of life abundant.

Dancing is dangerous. Thanks be to God! Amen.

20

ECSTATIC FOLLOWING

Imagine a drummer beginning to drum. Everyone starts tapping and clapping and moving. Being part of something bigger than us, the spontaneous parade, the spirited crowd, the song that rises out of nowhere, is magic. A Chinese proverb proclaims, "Not the cry, but the flight of the wild duck leads the flock to fly and follow." To be transported beyond individualism, two things must occur; someone must start something physical, and others must follow. Follow-the-leader is a core, universal activity for the whole human race. The more physical it is, the more fun.

Not a mere child's game, following and leading is how we bond to each other. We follow and lead in ceremonies, worship, and in court, where one person stands and everyone follows suit. Parents lead. A mother takes her bath and turns to find her children right behind her. Even babies lead. We can't help following their movements, squinching our face, and changing our voices to match theirs. Scientific studies show that the ability of infant and parent to physically interplay with appropriate ease, sharing cues of give-and-take, is pivotal to the developmental needs of early childhood.

The first time I met my husband, Stephen, we were at a wedding reception. Even though he says he was intimidated by my being a dancer, he asked me to dance. As our arms connected and we began, I felt my body looking for leadership and felt my impulse to provide it. I asked, "Who's leading?" He sheepishly smiled and we went from there.

The question, "Who's leading?" remains a theme of our marriage. My energetic, physical tendencies to initiate, and his gentler tendencies to follow or flow with me, are part of our daily dance. I have learned that leading is helpful, but not always by the same person. My physical impulse to initiate prevents me from experiencing the leading of others. The enduring question for an out-of-control leader such as myself is, "How well am I following?"

The dance of following and leading in partnership is sometimes subtle, sometimes overbearing. Sometimes it creates conflict, and sometimes perfect alchemy. Choice and physical awareness in dancing our relationships makes a huge difference. If we were to listen to our bodies, we would find that how we connect with each other comes out of deeply physical ways of being.

Phil and I believe that far too much emphasis is placed on leadership in our culture, and far too little on the power of "followership." There is no communal play if there are no followers. Following is what makes a communal body. Following is part of what makes families function. And in spiritual traditions disciple literally means to follow or to go with. Following does not mean subservience. It is a form of honouring whatever we enjoy and believe in by reinforcing it with our own body's "Yes!"

PARTNERED PLAY: FOLLOW FOR FUN

Follow the movements and sounds of a baby or child to empower their creativity and to reinforce their leadings. It's not important that you mirror their movements exactly. Following in the spirit of their movement is what is important. It is best if you let yourself feel and enjoy the movements you are following. Have them for yourself. As you do this, see if the leader will pick up on cues and follow you, too.

Follow a stranger without him knowing it. You can do this with the subtlest of movements. Notice your ability to pay attention, attune to them, and build on their leading.

———

Everyone leads. Every person has "stuff" to contribute. We use the general word "stuff" in Inter-Play to demystify creative impulses. We're not looking for good ideas or interesting ideas, just stuff: movements, sounds, words, ideas, images. Creative impulses often come from where we least expect them and from people who are just as happy to follow. Interesting creations emerge when a person's sense of direction is followed.

———

MEDITATION: "PLAY," *LIKE BREATHING*, #11

Listen to "Play." It is a goofy example of vocal "stuff." Notice that an idea begins and people follow and build on it. One small piece of input can start a whole snowball. Of course, you don't have to be as goofy as this, but if you let yourself, you will discover your ability to create on the spot with others. This is a revelation to many of us, strangely rewarding, and better than a thousand meetings.

———

PARTNERED PRACTICE: FOLLOW AND LEAD

Have one person be the leader and one be the follower for 30 seconds. Use only subtle movements. Change roles. Use fast movements. What do you notice from following or leading?

Every person can lead. Every person can follow. Once we begin to create with others, following binds the wondrous improvisational collage we know as community. Phil and I celebrate those with a gift for ecstatic following. People that follow particularly well are what we call "glue people." Their enthusiastic following mysteriously oils and knits the inner workings of all the relationships. They are often jokesters, cookie-bringers, huggers, and those who just know how to keep showing up.

Most people tend to follow with suspicion. However, learning to be an ecstatic follower can make a huge difference in community life. Instead of responding with reservation and hesitation, you and I can say "yes" in an embodied way to the leadings of others. It turns up the creative, communal heat and gets things cooking. It doesn't mean you have to do things exactly like the leader. Matching a leader's fullness with your own spirit is gift enough.

In a church I attended, I chose to enthusiastically follow the minister even though I never joined a committee. Instead of remaining preoccupied with my own ideas and concerns whenever I was sitting in the pew, I dedicated myself to sharing my spirit, verbally affirming him when I was moved, and showing up for things he initiated. I recognized that he couldn't lead every individual and released my need to have him do so. I thought of it as an energetic tithe of myself to his leading and the church. I didn't lose myself in doing this. In fact, I noticed that I had more fun at church than usual. I must say that following him wasn't hard. I enjoyed and admired his leadership, an important criteria for all committed following. I can't confirm how my commitment to ecstatically follow that minister made a difference in that church, but I suspect it did. To make a difference is a way of leading one's life. At that church, I learned a new and powerful form of leading – leading by following.

Questioning, criticizing, and withdrawing our energy in groups is rampant. The downside is that we are losing our sense of communal embodiment and health. Community and belonging is physical. Most people need to feel physically connected to people in order to sustain their sense of well-being. If you want to feel like you are more a part of your world, find people to follow. Physically attune yourself to your environment.

PARTNERED PLAY: FOLLOWING AS MEDITATION: "KYRIE,"
***LIKE BREATHING*, #8**

Have one person move their arm to lead with slow movement for a minute. When you follow, treat this like a visual meditation. Physically listen with your whole body. Go with this in quiet attainment. Without words, you may trade roles at any time. Do this with music if you choose.

When you follow others, it is common to use your eyes to follow your partner. This is both pleasant and limiting. You do not want to have to depend on being able to see to follow with spirit. Repetition liberates us from "eye co-dependency," always having to keep an eye on a leader in order to follow. Good leaders repeat themselves. This repetition helps followers integrate ideas more deeply into their own experience. Ideas become collective, embodied by the whole group in the process.

PARTNERED PLAY: FOLLOW IN RHYTHM

One person initiates a movement in a way that both people can easily repeat over and over for 30 seconds or more. Involve your voice if you like. Follow this. Change to a new repeating movement. Change roles. What do you notice?

Rhythm and repetition free both leader and follower from constantly having to come up with new ideas. The rhythm of two bodies moving together builds momentum and energy. Chanting, cheering, ritual, tradition, technique, and practice create a communal base of embodied experience. A security forms in group repetition that allows us to open up to deeper and wider parts of ourselves.

PARTNERED PLAY: FOLLOW WITH YOUR WHOLE BEING

Let go of having to directly look at your partner. Have one person initiate a repeatable movement. While both of you maintain the pattern, turn away, release eye contact and keep the movement going. Experiment with peripheral vision. Can you release your concern about following exactly or even well? You won't lose any points if your following is a beat behind. What counts is your ability to get on board and to get physically and playfully in tune.

Using your easy focus, you will start to notice that your body can follow changes instinctively. While this involves sight, your kinesthetic sense is a significant player in following and leading. Whether you are in close proximity or far apart, looking in the same direction, opposite, or in random directions, you can begin to co-create almost effortlessly. It feels like you are trusting your body to respond.

If you cannot physically replicate your partner's movements, it doesn't matter. We don't need exactness. Alter ideas to work for you. All adaptations are forms of following. One of our favourite InterPlayers, Megan Shirle, performs with Wing It! Performance Ensemble, and has muscular dystrophy with severely restricted arm and body movement. In fact, she laughingly says she hates hand dances. But she is able to alter and adapt all of her movement to fully communicate the experience of following. There is no question about her beauty, grace, or creativity as she follows and leads alongside the most able-bodied dancers. Conformity is not community. Willingness to join into the spirit of things is.

Having led and followed, do you notice a preference? Some of us are constant initiators. We barely know we are initiating because we do it so naturally. As a leader, I notice that I can only get my ideas to go as far as others are willing to follow. If I initiate too much, I become a soloist rather than a community builder. For balance, I follow others as a spiritual discipline. As you can imagine, my husband and my collaborator Phil both thank me.

Following doesn't mean giving up on my ideas or sense of self. In fact, the best followership involves the whole-hearted willingness to entertain, play with, and take in the ideas of others in order to have them for yourself. Indi Deickgrafe, a dance professor, does this magnificently. To her, following is like taking a trip into another land. You just get on and go, grateful for detours and the new views you get while experiencing the movements of others.

I look for both the spirit of followership and the willingness to lead in all of the people I play with. At the best of times, following and leading flows between us. Follower and leader aren't fixed roles. You can move beyond the question of "who is leading?" to notice that our ideas or actions are what is actually leading. Where there is reciprocal creative flow, enjoyment prevails, new ideas and dreams come easily, and a feeling of wellness rushes in.

PARTNERED PLAY: FOLLOWING IDEAS TOGETHER

Let one partner start while the other follows. As you play, let the leadership shift between the two of you (without using words or signals). Release yourselves from a strict leader role. Instead, follow the ideas of either partner as they come. You don't even have to make sure each person is getting their fair share of leading. Sharing equally is not as important as creating something satisfying together. Many people enjoy the role of following ideas. If you can't find the place where it feels easy and ideas (or something else) seem to be leading, don't worry. Let it go. Sometimes the particular time or energy between partners doesn't lend itself to this. Notice what else is there. Is there fun in just following or just leading?

——-·—

When we are in spontaneous interchange, led by the surprise of information and ideas in the moment, our interplay can be one of the easiest, most pressure-free forms of partnering. It can be sheer unspeakable grace. The focus is not on the creativity of individuals as much as it is on what the creation needs. Ideas flow. Like good conversation, one thing builds on another. A physical communion wells up in us. Something bigger happens. This transcendence is a dance where we become more than dancers and players. We are the danced.

——-·—

"INCREDIBLY, INTIMIDATINGLY,
THE WORDS 'PERFORMERS' AND 'COMMUNITY ARTISTS'
JOIN 'TEACHERS' AND 'ORGANIZATIONAL CONSULTANTS'
ON OUR BUSINESS CARD."

TOM HENDERSON AND GINNY GOING

never expected that what the body wants would be
the dominant theme of their retirement years,
their new marriage, and their business.

Ginny: She is 6 years old, performing in a first-grade play. It's being held outdoors; a blanket hanging over a clothesline is the stage backdrop. She's memorized her lines and her mother tells later how she also memorized and mouthed the lines of all the other characters throughout the play.

Tom: As a child, he falls asleep at night listening to his father play the banjo. In 3rd grade, he rehearses for the school production of *Peer Gynt*; he does "gobliny" things in the "Hall of the Mountain King" – loving it! The day before the performance, the teacher says, "Now don't any of you get stage fright on me." The next day he dissolves in a puddle of perceived incompetence and shame.

Ginny: At age 9, she sings in the junior choir of St. George's Episcopal Church in Arlington, Virginia. She doesn't read music but memorizes it by ear. When the choir takes part in a huge festival at the National Cathedral in Washington, D.C., her body is flooded with joy at the sound of her voice joining hundreds of others swirling high into the cathedral's arches and vaults.

Tom: At 16, he organizes a dance band, plays alto sax with Bert Lewis on trumpet, Brickle Reese on guitar, Al Koenigsberg on drums, and Al Hills on bass. Playing at dances, he feels competent, powerful, "on stage," yet somehow anonymous, surprised when other students recognize him. Otherwise, he is shy. Speaking in front of others, even telling jokes to a group of friends, he is awkward, uncomfortable. Dancing is excruciatingly painful. He envies tall "Cal" Calvacchio, whose long legs carry him effortlessly across the gymnasium floor with partner, Martha. He is too clumsy to ever learn the steps. If actually attending a dance, Tom and his partners spend most of the time in feigned rapt attention to the band.

Ginny: At 16, she's introduced to modern dance by a high school gym teacher. She uses her babysitting money to take classes on her own, but feels too awkward and embarrassed to take part in the recital. The other students have been taking classes for years and she's too far behind.

Tom: At 31, he has long since given up the saxophone and most other fun pursuits as well. Ideas of dancing are light years distant. Life is serious. He is a husband, a father of two daughters, a chemistry post-doc, responsible, ambitious. In college, he spent a blessed year in Germany, forced by the difficulty of mastering German and science at the same time, to relax temporarily into German drama and poetry. Now, presenting a seminar to a group of graduate students, he quotes a line from Schiller. Afterwards, his advisor says, "If you're such a poet, Tom, why not write a poem for Jorge who is leaving." With only a little prodding, he accepts, gathers the dirt on Jorge, writes a bit of doggerel. At the same time, he writes his first serious poetry – seven lines about his seven-year-old daughter.

Ginny: By age 45, she carries so many stories in her body – of marriage at 21, pregnancies, miscarriages, babies grown to adulthood, careers, mid-life craziness, divorce, spiritual upheaval, ordination, a new relationship with exciting, scary possibilities. It's like an underground river of lava ready to burst out. But where and how? She has spent much of her life energy focussed outward – figuring out the rules and following them, to create a box of safety in a world lacking welcome and space for her from the time she was very small.

Tom: In mid-life, in the midst of a devastating affair, the guilt and pain of separation and divorce, it is, surprisingly, an aerobic dance class that saves his life. It's harder to be depressed while moving like this – especially in the company of others. He decides he needs more play in his life, and for a while works very hard at having more.

Ginny: Exploring her sexuality, spiritual direction, falling in love with unlikely people who mirror what she can't yet see in herself, therapy, discovering women as friends, deciding she was a "good enough" mother. The lava begins to move – not a flow at first, just small amounts bubbling up through cracks here and there. She takes a huge leap from a 15-year friendship into an intimate partnership with a man for whom she glimpses enormous possibilities – and giant barriers to building a life together.

Tom: It's too soon. It's awkward. They've been friends for 15 years, their children have grown up together – the same church, the same social circles. She is nearing ordination as a deacon in the Episcopal Church. There is an anonymous complaint to the bishop from a member of the congregation. There is, nevertheless, something right and good here, something not to be relinquished.

They are passionate about the same things. They are equals, meet each other, hold their ground, don't back away. He the introverted scientist, deep thinker, gentle, quiet, calm; she the extroverted organizer, a deep feeler, pushy and energetic – two streams of lava flowing side by side and crisscrossing back and forth, heading, God knows where, to what ocean, to form what new ground?

Spirit leads sneakily, one step at a time, the lava picks up speed. The poem Tom writes to celebrate their wedding includes the lines: "come I bid you, chance with me / what new music God may play / and if you will, then you and I shall dance / while songs go on…" Dancing together is still more metaphor than fact. But in the first year of their marriage, a workshop on "Sexuality and Spirituality: The Travail of Integration" introduces them to the joy and release of creative movement. "There is no wrong way to do this" is unexpectedly compelling.

A dancing priest friend tells of experiencing something new called InterPlay in California. They do a body wisdom workshop with Phil and Cynthia at the Pacific School of Religion. On Thursday night, there is an informal performance. Sign up beforehand if you want, but no one has to. Still, "there may be some surprises." They don't, of course, sign up. Surprise! Cynthia calls them out to do an improvisational following and leading dance to "Money" from Cabaret. Impossible! – but not impossible!

The lava pops and sizzles and occasionally sends up huge showers of fire. They discover step by step, together and separately, who they are as creative, embodied artists. They take on "affirmation" and "going with" as life practices. They try to remember to breathe. They expand and explode their pictures of what they can have and what they can create together. Phil and Cynthia keep saying "yes, yes, yes." They are still waiting for the "no" that never comes!

And then the biggest surprise of all. Having come to InterPlay through the door of personal growth / spiritual transformation, they decide to create a performance with some improvising playmates in honour of Susanna, a friend from California. No blanket hanging over a clothesline as a backdrop, but the flavour is the same! Friends are invited and come – 50 of them! Off The Deep End Ensemble is born. Incredibly, intimidatingly, the words "performers" and "community artists" join "teachers" and "organizational consultants" on their business card. Importantly, making very public art – stories, songs, dances – out of life's stuff provides a way to deal with and transform it.

And the most recent and perhaps most satisfying "yes" is the gift of affirming and mentoring others who are drawn to the possibility of leading a more embodied life and discovering the deep flow of creativity within them – people who sometimes change their lives in scary and inspiring ways.

The red, hot lava flows within each of us – dangerous, powerful, beautiful. The artist, singer, storyteller, dancer waits to emerge, ready to take each of us beyond our wildest dreams. Yes, yes, yes!

21

JOYOUS DIVERSITY, PEACE THROUGH PLAY

We bought InterPlayce, a two-story building in downtown Oakland, and converted it into a large studio dedicated to creativity, community, and change. It's on the edge of what neighbours call "Little Korea." Across the street is Sunny's Korean beauty shop and an African-American gay bar. A Buddhist Temple is to the right and an apartment building for those living with AIDS and other long-term illnesses is around the corner. Kitty corner, a Gen-X northern European gal runs the Mama Buzz Café and art gallery. This is our cultural milieu.

One vibrant Sunday morning, walking to the building, a handsome, 30ish black man with coiled hair and a few lost teeth came my way, singing. We met with our eyes, smiling. Twenty steps past each other, we both turned and looked back. His singing changed to blessing. He was singing me up and down, and walked right back up to me. Homeless, a little crazy, and hungry? At that moment, his song was at the top of the charts. The space between us was alive. Our mutual willingness to play with that space made it more so. It reminded me that the word entertain means to hold between.

How do we allow for cultural difference and still get to our universal communion? First, diverse people need to show up in the same places. This is easier than we think. No two bodies are alike. No two stories or histories are the same. Though we have been taught to downplay being different, diversity is our birthright. We are born different. This is especially true in the United States. Except for native peoples, we are a nation of immigrants, movers. You might presume that everyone in a room full of people is the same, but if you do a little storytelling you'll uncover amazing worlds of difference. Who we are related to, where we came from, how we do the simple things of life: our diversity is as close as our ordinary acts of living. When we reveal the details of our lives to each other, differences are revealed and we can begin to celebrate them.

PARTNERED PLAY:
REVEAL THE WONDERFUL, HIDDEN ORDINARY

Using the easy-focus way of babbling, do some short "tellings" with a partner or partners. Take 30 seconds each to tell about your families' mealtimes, gardening, a favourite holiday time, something you've inherited, a relative, what kind of work your family ancestors did. Describe things in physical detail. That's where the differences reveal themselves.

Although I had thought of myself as an "open," friendly person, for years I had relatively few relationships with people of different ethnic and religious backgrounds. I wondered how this could be since I was surrounded by diversity. Investigating my life and experimenting with multicultural interplay, I developed a theory that, in order for there to be a world of peace, we need to come out and play together. Of course, this would require that others want to play with me and that I want to play with them. That is when I started praying for new friends and to turn the ship of my white thinking and behaviours toward new ports.

I believe peace can only be achieved when there is a mutual desire for relationship. Relationship has play at its heart. Provoke play and relationship begins. You can be sneaky about this. Play is like that. It takes attention off of us and puts it on creating something. Creating a connection with someone is play. Chat with a stranger in the grocery line. Open a door with a playful gesture. Sometimes to remember someone's name I emphasize it. "Dave!" I exclaim as I smile. Oddly, I become more connected to Dave over time, repeating his name in a similar way when we meet. He smiles. If he didn't, I'd drop it.

Someone said play is the opposite of war. In multi-ethnic, interfaith community building, we tend to spend our time problem-solving and putting out the fires of conflict. No one wants to be seen as a problem. Have we tried to change or fix situations or peoples before we have created a basis for love and community? A tendency to emphasize helping people and fixing social problems does not attract playmates. To play with people requires a willingness to shake off seeing everything as a problem and a readiness to be transformed by people, their stories, and their beauty.

As the war on terrorism began in the 21st century, playing together has become more urgent for me. Struggling with war, in a letter to the InterPlay community I wrote the following:

What if the absolute best way to love is through play? What if the most magical strategies for world peace are lying out in the backyard, like so many forgotten childhood toys and all we have to do is go out the back door for five minutes to see what's there?

As an activist, my work to change the world is to play. I make beauty and love, strive to be perfectly honest every day, and encourage others to do the same. This is slow work. But the good news is that it is working. In the middle of a country in crisis, I find health and hope around me. I think heaven wants me to stick with this. While I am part of wider, nonviolent interventions, and support those who run wildly into and against governmental urgencies to overthrow and attack, I uphold my actions as more than demonstration – it is play. With those holding their banners, their computers, their songs, and their strategies for systematic denouncement of all that is incompatible with the Great Body's Health, I am here too – leaning into the wind of anguish and refusing to give up. I am dancing in the parade. In days to come, I am going to wear pink and stand with women who stay in love amidst the potholes and mine fields of distress…because loving is living.

How do we find diverse playmates? All of us have location ruts, particularly Caucasians. We move toward our familiar cultural group quicker than anyone. In the adventure of multicultural InterPlay, the first step is to come out and play. To do this we only have to leave our own house. Diversity is probably all around us: at the grocery store, at the gas station, in the office, and at the toll booth as we cross the bridge. Meet the world with a spirit of play and pretty soon you have knit yourself into a new corner of the world.

Once together, we don't have to learn everything about each other's cultural backgrounds in order to begin. We are bodies: different and the same. Playing side by side allows serendipity and common experiences to weave their way through our following, leading, and beginning contact. We are free to dance our own dance and yet to be also together.

David, a tall African-American; and Beth, fair, blond; danced side by side in a mass dedicated to the archangels. Before the altar, they each moved in their own way while their tangible affection proclaimed two cultural forces sharing the same divine space. The image flung from the heart of the sanctuary that day said, "Black and white don't make gray – they explode in vibrant colour."

PARTNERED PLAY: DANCE SIDE BY SIDE: "ON BEHALF OF,"
LIKE BREATHING, **#14**

A good practice for developing a sense of awareness and ease in diverse relationships is to practice dancing side by side. With a partner, give each other room. Using easy focus, sense your partner, but don't attach to him or her directly. In fact, you can release your obligation to relate to them at all. Let the spirit around you hold you together. Dance side by side. Be full. Don't try to accommodate your partner. Let the space hold you both. If eye contact or relationship occurs, let it come. Enjoy it as a gift.

Releasing ourselves from the obligation to relate directly takes huge burdens of expectation off of us. Interracial and interfaith relationships are particularly complex. Political correctness can often supersede authentic body-to-body communication. If we can let go a little, our bodies often go right to the place spirit and unity live, where all things dance together. This is not to dismiss the reluctance to play that people of colour may feel toward Caucasians, or that one group may feel for another. People of colour are frequently hurt by white cultures. I know when I've been hurt by someone I don't feel like playing with them. However, as a white person, my commitment to multicultural InterPlay is to embrace colourfulness as the deepest good and to keep showing up to play and love even if I am rejected. I do this because I long for the grace of the whole body, in all of our colour and diversity.

Community building often focuses on big themes, but it turns out that it is sharing little things that weave our differences together. Intimacy comes through meals, dancing, music, and stories. Telling stories side by side is like making a story collage. Partners let fragments of each of their stories emerge, piecing them together freely like a crazy quilt.

Unlike normal social interchange where listening to each other is the key, in side-by-side stories, the players allow their easy focus and the bigger picture to hold it all. Relaxing enough to let our stories come out side by side is the goal. Interruption and layering is a necessary part of it. We let go of the primacy of hearing all parts of each individual voice. This is group play. Overhearing a partner's story may influence and provoke us, or we may find ourselves solidly standing in our own truth. Instead of competing for time and space, the tellers focus outward, toward the audience. Side by side, our energy goes into making something surprising together.

PARTNERED PLAY: SIDE-BY-SIDE STORIES

A little warning: This is considered a more advanced InterPlay form. We are not used to using words in such an overlapping, musical way.

Side by side, both partners simultaneously babble about newspapers for 30 seconds. Think of your voices as an orchestra, rather than as competing solo instruments. Babble again for a minute about trees, with each person introducing their own random pauses. This reveals moments where only one voice is heard. Loosen your hold on making meaning and play with letting sound and meaning co-exist. Your two tellings needn't be equal in time, style, or content. Words can be unrelated. Just stay connected to your own telling through-out. If you are in a situation where you can listen to two people speaking side by side, you will notice that a lot of the meaning comes through.

I like to imagine that listening to and participating in side-by-side stories is like listening from God's point of view. In truth, all of us are talking at the same time in an incredible collage of human experience. We can play with this as part of our reality. Playing side by side honours differences, while framing them together. This can be surprisingly freeing and healing.

Sobunfu Some's book on African healing rituals, *The Spirit of Intimacy*, tells of a ritual for marriage in which a couple sits back to back inside a circle drawn on the earth. They simulta-neously, loudly, complain to God about injuries inflicted upon them by the other in the daily course of household life. The higher power is their witness. Both parties stick with it until their grievances are said. As it becomes evident that there is literally more than one side to the story, each partner, though unobligated to listen to the other, can't help but hear the com-plaint of the other.

Couples, friends, strangers, and even enemies need freedom to relate side by side in their truths. All truths do not need to merge or resolve into a common statement. In a multicultural InterPlay performance, Malka, daughter of Polish Jewish im-migrants, and Jurgen, son of working-class German parents, placed personal histories alongside each other and danced through each other's space. They both talked about their mother in very different ways, when suddenly, Jurgen, speaking of his mom, lifted 50-year-old Malka into the air. She arched back, her wild Jewish hair spinning in ecstatic flight. In that moment, history rearranged itself. Who was the mother?

Two weeks after the New York World Trade Center attacks, Amar Khalsa, a Wing It! Performance Ensemble musician and an American Sikh, rose to chant at our concert. Twelve of us silently stood alongside him as he spoke of his fear for his son's safety. As Amar sang the wisdom of the ages in a prayer of peace for us all, just standing alongside him onstage told our deeper story. Solidarity is physically standing with another.

Katrina Browne's ancestors ran slave ships out of Bristol, Rhode Island. Juanita Brown is an African-American dancer and educational consultant. In a film called *Traces of the Trade: A Story from the Deep North*, Katrina and Juanita worked together to document the journey of some of Katrina's family, retracing the slave route of family ships to West Africa and Cuba. During the process, I was invited to the Bristol Historical and Preservation Society to offer InterPlay as a resource. We sighed, shook out anxiety, babbled, danced hand-to-hand, and played with walking, stopping, and running. The transformative moment came in witnessing Katrina and Juanita improvisationally dance and speak their stories side by side, black and white, revealing their connection and anguish in tackling the agony of slavery. Because of that dance, Katrina's family knew something deeper and yet unspeakable about why they each had come. These two women – different histories, different races – held a holy fire between them.

Play changes both the individual and the world. It makes us both more unusual, more joyously diverse, and more hopeful. I believe play's time has come. Ranier Maria Rilke sensed this when he wrote, "Again and again people in the crowd wake up... They carry strange customs with them and demand room for bold gestures. The future speaks ruthlessly though them."

"A SOLIDARITY THAT NO WORDS CAN ARTICULATE FILLED THE ROOM."

MASANKHO BANDA

who came to the United States as a political refugee
from Malawi, Africa, became an artist, activist, and teacher for
peace in dance, song, and story.

I was dancing on the edge of the world. It was upstate New York, late spring 2000. Everything was green and there was intermittent rain still falling. The Maryknoll Mission Association of the Faithful invited me to facilitate the stories held in their heads and to move them into their bodies. I cherished this assignment. I would be able to answer the call grandmother gave me when I was five years old to grow up using dance and music to heal spirits and bring peace.

Meeting the attendees I realized the enormity of my task. Lay missionaries, serving people all over the world, had arrived in New York full of anguish, despair, hopelessness, and sometimes outright anger. In three weeks they would return to their work with AIDS orphans and women infected with HIV / AIDS in Africa; with street children sniffing glue in Brazil; with women battered by alcoholic husbands in Venezuela; with resistance fighters in Chiapas, Mexico; with refugees and child soldiers in the Sudan; and with prostitutes and sex slaves in Asia. As each person introduced themself, I felt my bodyspirit sink lower and lower into the ground. What could I do to help?

Calling upon the resources of my ancestry, I knew that the first thing for me to do was to call in the elements and the ancestors. This was a task bigger than the 50 of us gathered in the room. It was necessary to reach beyond the confines of the beautiful conference centre, to extend into the green leaves, the waters of the rivers of the area, and the rich brown soil of the surrounding fields. The ancestors were ready to be awakened to join us and give us strength.

I gathered us all into a circle and took out my drum. I was ready. I scanned the expectant faces around me. It was hard to tell. Some seemed ready, others appeared resigned, and a few were downright skeptical. I was warned about one participant. Watch out for him, he doesn't care much for you California touchy-feely people. I took a deep breath, and after teaching them the simple chant "Baba Yo," we launched into hearty singing and dancing as we called in the ancestors. For a full three minutes we sang and danced as my hands danced on my djembe. As the drum notes died down I looked around the room and realized that already a shift was happening. Everybody had participated. We were on our way.

Not wanting to let the momentum drop, I walked to my CD player where the song "Adjaja" (Invocation of the elements), by Baba Tunde Olatunji, was already in the player and hit the start key. I led the participants through the fire, water, air, and earth invocation dance explaining that in Africa the best way to take care of our planet was to become our planet through dance. Only when earth, water, air, and fire are an integral part of who are can we responsibly take care of the planet and each other. Perceptions were beginning to shift. Already, the lay missionaries began to speak of a kinship and connection with each other that they had not felt at previous assemblies. Two songs, drums and dancing for ten minutes, and the magic was cast. I was blessed to be a channel for energies beyond me to come through.

All participants had stories to share of the work that they were doing around the world. With their desire to share their stories in a way that would renew and empower them and inspire and encourage their fellow missionaries, I taught them how to tell Interplay Big Body Stories – telling their story from their whole body. By the end of the day, the participants retired for the night as excited as children on Christmas morning sitting in living rooms strewn with toys. They had new tools. They understood that in the midst of anguish, despair, anger, and frustration, they had a way of getting through to the other side that was easy and, dare they admit it, fun.

In the days that followed, their stories and dances changed us all. Two women who were working with street children in Brazil stole our hearts. Dressed like street children and talking in the language of street, a mixture of English, Portuguese, and the local Brazilian language, they had in their hands brown paper bags folded at the top. They showed us dances the kids perform to get money to buy glue and paint to put in the brown paper bags to sniff. Then they showed us the youth dancing under the influence of the glue and paint, and spoke in drug-induced slurred language. We watched as the kids high on glue ran into the arms of the volunteers and would not let go. In the midst of pain, the kids knew love even when it was before their drug-crazed eyes. With tears in our eyes and empowered by what we had just witnessed, I led everyone in a dance on behalf of all the children who are abandoned to live alone on the streets around the world. We danced our frustrations with government systems and communities that allow this injustice to happen. We closed with a dance of intention. We set our intentions in our bodies, to gather strength from each other to help these and other children around the world.

Having just returned from Africa, I resonated with the presentation of missionaries from Kenya. With video, slides, and dances, they shared their volunteer work with people infected with HIV / AIDS, affecting possibly one out of ten or even one out of five Kenyans. It is local musicians who have the most impact on AIDS education. We danced to songs that they had learned. It was exhilarating. With tears in our eyes, we watched scenes of women and men dying alone, abandoned by family members because of fear of infection. I had never imagined a person so weak that they could not lift a cup to their mouth to drink, dying from thirst. We closed with a dance of grieving for the departed, and a dance for healing and finding a cure. All these dances were to African music. I started out leading and then everyone evolved the dances into their own expressions, dancing from our heart movements coming from the earth and from our ancestors. A sense of solidarity that no words can articulate filled the room. In our bodies we felt we could find a cure for HIV / AIDS.

For three days, we travelled around the world as each group presented through dance, big-body stories, slides, and video stories. Each day to wrap up, an incredible poet wrote free verse and haikus based on what he was hearing, seeing, and feeling. I improvised in dance and story. Our spontaneous side-by-side interchange wove together everything that had been shared. We took what *was* and turned it into what could *be*. Taking people's stories, tears, fears, and hopes and giving them back in this embodied form was an incredible gift. Even skeptics at the beginning of the week were fully converted.

That week we went through incredible transformations. People crossed oceans to come together in a conference centre in upstate New York. The stories we carried in our bodies, stories that make up our incredible multicultural life, moved, healed, and gave way to joy. We learned we can dance at the borders and edges of our world.

PLAY THAT HEALS

22

PLAY HEALS

I disagree with Ecclesiastes. There isn't a time for mourning and a time for dancing. Suffering is not the opposite of play and creation. It's a part of it. To have full-time grace, we must dance it all. I know because I recently made a list of all the things I have healed by playing with them: all the things that have offered themselves up to me in playing. In seminary, I discovered the lamentations of the prophet Jeremiah. He was intensely angry at God for his prophetic ministry. He accused God of raping him and of leaving him alone to carry a yoke of rage. For Old Testament class, I made a dance called Yoke of Rage, as I experimented and threw myself into the impossible tension of God and humanity, one arm reaching toward earth and the other crossed and reaching toward heaven. Looking back, I see that the rage that I was playing out for myself and my family of origin was being creatively valued for the first time.

Suffering must dance. In an April 1923 letter reflecting on the world's tragedies, Ranier Maria Rilke wrote the following.

It is true that these mysteries are dreadful, and people have always drawn away from them. But where can we find anything sweet and glorious that would never wear this mask of the dreadful? Whoever does not sometime or another give his full consent, his full and joyous consent to the dreadfulness of life, can never take full possession of the unutterable abundance and power of our existence, can only walk on its edge, and one day, when the judgment is given, will have been neither alive nor dead.

In the apocryphal *Acts of John*, Jesus sings to his disciples and says, "Learn to suffer so as not to suffer." Resisting the body of struggle does not lead us to the playground, nor does getting stuck in problem-solving and healing. We must learn to have the suffering right in the mix of our play if we are to transform each moment into something glorious.

Scratch the surface of any spiritual tradition and there is the body recreating itself. You can find it in *davaning*, the Jewish prayer form of rocking as one prays; in perfecting physical meditations on power and surrender in the martial arts; and in the circling and stomping, swaying and pounding in the Pacific Islands, Africa, and ancient Europe. Jesus healed, lifted bodies, and called his followers in challenging, confusing times to "rejoice and leap for joy" (Luke 6:23). And, on the worst night of all, in the *Acts of John* it says that he asked his disciples to form a ring, to dance and sing, "Glory be to thee God, Glory be to thee Grace. Grace dances, dance ye all. Who does not dance? Does not know what comes to pass." Grace plays hardest in the darkest nights.

The fastest road to healing may be play. More and more people find the expressive arts to be a radical way to move their body and imagination toward health. Playing, dancing, singing, and creating are not just for recreation. Michael Miller, InterPlayer, says, "Play is for when your life is all up in a heaval."

To dance through difficulty requires enough community support, the right methods for what ails us, and spiritual help.

This must be how Nelson Mandela and Desmond Tutu in South Africa danced through collective anger and sorrow to liberation – by reaching with the whole bodyspirit and going deeper than ideology, deeper than policy, deeper than competition, to the source of enduring inspiration. That is where grace lifts us from the ashes. Again, when the poet Rainer Maria Rilke was asked, "But the deadly and the violent days, how do you undergo them, take them in?" he answered, "I praise."

Nancy Brink has had chronic back pain and arthritis since her teen years. If she only listened to pain she would stop everything. However, dancing, writing poetry, and swimming take her to a more timeless, bigger body, the place in the body that many healers invoke to transform illness.

Denise found Interplay when she was in recovery from cancer and surgery. She discovered InterPlay and a band of people whose dreams were telling them to dance in order to heal. Through this she was inspired to leap up on a stage, to move, and to tell her own story of cancer and health.

Creativity is miraculously regenerative, simple and accessible. Creativity heals. Play heals. Margaret Wheatley and Myron Keller-Rogers, in their book *A Simpler Way*, suggest that

The simpler way summons forth the best about us. It asks us to understand human nature differently, more optimistically. It identifies us as creative. It acknowledges that we seek after meaning. It asks us to be less serious, yet more purposeful, about our work and our lives. It does not separate play from the nature of being.

Instead of attacking problems, play works homeopathically. Play welcomes woundedness without making a huge deal out of it all. Play concentrates upon and elevates wholeness rather than weakness. Artists who discover this give rise to songs, paintings, dances, and scripts that play out the vulnerability of their lives. Duke Ellington said, "I merely took the energy it takes to pout and wrote some blues." You can too.

Play heals in part because it takes the pressure off of what hurts. Our bodies love to create. Play activates the best in us for nothing but recreation. In recreation we are created anew. Our creative energy, like a tide of health, sweeps our challenges in the direction of well-being.

Four specific ways play heals include

1. exformation – moving out what hurts us or is not necessary
2. retrieval – bringing parts of our experience back into our body
3. restoration – rebuilding our bodyspirits through nurture, and
4. maintaining health – playing just because it feels good.

In exformation, as I mentioned in Chapter 11, "The Power of Feeling," we find we can move out a lot of the emotional and energetic stuff that our bodyspirits accumulate. Feelings, thoughts, messages, and memories all need to move. So do the impressions that we collect from other people and from the media. We are not obligated to carry all the concerns of the world. In addition, we can move our own highest wisdom out into the light where we can see it. The expressive arts are remarkable in their ability to help us reveal things to ourselves about ourselves. But more than awareness occurs. We are somehow also lightening our load.

PLAY: DANCE TO EXFORM AND DISCERN "TURBAN BLUES,"
***LIKE BREATHING*, #18**

Bring a question or challenge and use your imagination to place it into the space in front of you. It could be an emotional, vocational, relational, or medical challenge. With your easy focus, release attempts to understand or work at healing or discerning in this moment. You can really let go of the question once you begin. Now let one hand move freely accompanied by music. Let the dance lead you. Just play and see what comes. Afterward, reflect on how the dance might be a response to your question.

———

Anytime we reclaim an activity or aspect of life that brings us grace we are practicing soul retrieval. Angeles Arrien, a well-known spiritual teacher, reminds us what indigenous people know: that anyone who stops singing their own song, dancing their own dance, telling their own stories, or who has lost the ability to be still, loses their soul. InterPlay is a soul-retrieving activity because it teaches adults and children incremental steps that give them back these things.

I have seen people begin to weep the first moment they were allowed to dance freely again. On the other hand, one woman told me that she literally froze when she started to do a hand dance. She could not move. It troubled her that such a basic freedom was not available to her so she began the journey of healing by finding a teacher who could go slowly and compassionately with her as she retrieved this ability one play at a time.

I also think we lose ourselves every day. In our hectic world, we feel scattered and stretched. Our awareness moves from the far corners of the world to daycare to our desk. Many people use the language, "I'm not in my body." Playing is one of the most gracious, easy ways to come home to ourselves.

———

PLAY: GATHER YOUR SPIRIT HOME

Reach out your arms wide. Do you feel that your spirit is out there or closed in? Many of us feel scattered, all over the place. This may be truer than we realize. Reach behind you and using your kinesthetic imagination to playfully grab your spirit from all the places in the past that you might have left it. (You don't have to consciously know where.) Gather your spirit up to a place just over your head. Now reach into the future where you have been projecting your concerns and plans. Imaginatively grasp hold of your spirit and bring it over-head. Reach out to either side of you and gather yourself back from all of those you love and those you hate. Bring this energy back. Now with your hands on your energy over your head, bring your spirit back into your body. Squirm around in it. Give yourself the gift of dancing your spirit home. Dance grounds us in our body. Our bodyspirit likes nothing better than being affirmed in our own movement.

Retrieving parts of ourselves is possible through our rites of play. For times when we have lost precious parts of our identity and energy through trauma and abuse, the help of a trained guide and healer is needed. A wise, embodied person can dance, pray, sing, and follow spirit to the source of healing on our be-half. For many people, it is a relief to know that you don't have to re-traumatize yourself to get where you are going. This is incredible body wisdom.

Restoration includes all activities that return us to balance and ease: massage, aroma therapy, hugging, deep breathing. One of the most famous restorative practices in InterPlay is a surprising one. We call it the "evil twin." Our evil twin is the inclusion of the politically incorrect, wilder, bolder, more flir-tatious and raucous part of us. For those of us bent on being and doing good, the evil twin has a great role to play in restor-ing balance to our humourlessness.

Mary, an environmentalist, theologian, artist, and former biology teacher, knows perfectly well the virtues and thrills of her evil twin. She exformed this restorative advice to herself and me.

It's 4 a.m., Wednesday, September 26. I'm into the honking/rasping/sleepless stage of some spirited, organic human body virus. At least if you're a computer, your pet person can be warned not to open a file that reads, "Do you love porn?" or "Infamous Family Pictures." But we humans have to go unalerted through this ever more virulent world of microbes, it seems. Just 72 hours ago I was a (becoming) competent systematic theologian, with the blush of an InterPlayer pinking my cheeks. This a.m. I am more like mashed yeast: glowless and smushed single cell into single cell by zero gravity. In fact, right now someone is flying around the room with my very light head. I'm watching her from my bed. If this laptop weren't weighing down my feverish thighs, I would join her. I have actually made an important decision, curled up here in torment. I am going to let my evil twin write my master's thesis. I'll probably even let her write it from the ceiling where she is still flying around with my very light head. Be well and ever vigilant against viral contamination of all species. As a biologist, I must admit, the microbial world offers much resistance to unconditional love. Pax, Mary

Did I mention that Mary is a nun?

PLAY: YOUR EVIL TWIN

Some favourite evil-twin activities include the following:
- Whine loudly about something you dislike for 30 seconds.
- Stand on a chair and rant about world affairs, laundry, or anything else.
- Babble about your life purpose from the point of view of your evil twin.

- Speak in a made-up foreign language about something vital to you.

Try this and see what you notice. It's almost always more fun with a witness.

Lastly, play heals simply because it is fun. Fun heals. That's all there is to it. No one has to tell us to get back to play. Play is right at the base line. Albert Einstein had a mathematical formulation for success in life. He said, "If A = success, then A = x (play) + y (work) + z (knowing when to shut up)." We can edge our way toward refreshment every chance we get, though most of us can't figure out when to shut up.

It seems that those who play and who are embodied tend to judge less. Judgment isn't fun. Play honours gifts and limits without overemphasizing either. Playing isn't primarily concerned with changing or improving anyone or anything. Play takes people and the world on the terms given. I've read that the Dali Llama squirms around in his seat, laughs easily, and has always been very curious about the world. That's the kind of spiritual teacher I look for – one who knows how bad it can be and who can still play.

"UNCONDITIONAL LOVE IS NOT AN EASY THING
TO FIND IN THE WORLD TODAY, YET HERE IT IS
IN BRIGHT LIVING COLOURS."

SUSAN CUBEL

after dedicating herself to recovering life, faced a chronic illness.

Eight years ago I felt awkward, clumsy, inadequate, totally anxious and basically terrified. I was an expert at hiding all of my feelings. I never considered myself to be artistic in any way. But ever since I jumped into my body in my very first InterPlay class, I couldn't seem to get enough.

Then in February one year, after my doctor prescribed an antibiotic for a sinus infection, I proceeded to get a severe reaction. When I went back to see the doctor, I was misdiagnosed, told I had the flu and received additional medications along with the original antibiotic. As a result, my immune system was poisoned and my whole body went into shock. I almost died.

In the end, I contracted fibromyalgia, a widespread musculoskeletal pain and fatigue disorder for which the cause and cure is still unknown. I ache all over, my muscles twitch and throb with spasmodic pain as though I'm being stabbed, and my skin burns all of the time. I am devoid of energy as though my power supply is unplugged. I have difficulty concentrating for long periods and I have disturbed sleep. Other than that, I am just fine! Needless to say, I had written off ever having a normal life again, and this included InterPlay.

Now, 15 months later, I am full of joy because I am giving myself the gift of play, no matter how I feel. I have learned to honour my body and to participate fully regardless of the pain.

I am still sad and mourn my old body. I am angry that I have limitations due to the pain I experience. When I push myself too far, I pay for it in volumes of additional pain the following day, week, or month.

I am told that this disease is not curable, but that if I keep trying, I will eventually find a way to put it into remission. It's difficult to stay out of the frustration of it all. I am not a saint. To be a regular human being and to ask for help is such a humbling experience. But when I do the results are awesome.

So here I am, performing and playing again. I am a ham and love to be the centre of attention. The audience's smiling faces urge me on. I am doing what I love with my community supporting me as I support them. It is a miracle that I am even here integrated back into the InterPlay community, as though I had never left. As far as they were concerned, I was firmly and forever ensconced among them. It warms my heart and gives me energy and strength to continue.

Unconditional love is not an easy thing to find in the world today, yet here it is in bright living colours. It's in the hugs we share, in the dances we compose, in the words we communicate, in the stories we tell, and in the duets that we create together. I am forever grateful.

23

—

CREATING ON BEHALF OF OTHERS

Some devastations we face are bigger than we can stand. In 1998, someone significant to me died every six weeks. I call that year my doctorate in death. I know others with similar journeys. During the Vietnam War, one of my friends escaped his country by boat losing all he possessed, including some of his family members. In that war, another friend of mine lost his entire platoon and was the only survivor.

When our difficulties are literally too great to bear, when we are too sick, too troubled, or too incapacitated to help ourselves, when we can't surmount suffering on our own, we need a community of folks to show up and do something physical on our behalf. In earlier times, that is when communal healing rituals occurred. Today, dancing, singing, and creating on behalf of others is still one of our most potent, yet under-used forms of social-spiritual intervention.

After the attack of September 11, everyone in the United States felt an unusually pronounced connection with each other. Our inter-kinesthetic suffering fueled the relentless hauling away of debris. Attending memorial after memorial, releasing and soothing each other, everyone felt the need to do something. This doing or undoing is a blessing. Margery Allingham says, "Mourning is not forgetting. It is an undoing. Every minute tie must be untied and something permanent and valuable recovered and assimilated from the dust." Jesus said, "Blessed are they who mourn for they shall be comforted."

Concrete physical action is a way of unmaking one circumstance and remaking it into another. We give blood, send money, raise flags, pray, bring food, and help neighbours. The need to physically exform grief and rage and to act on behalf of the group that is inside and outside of our bodies, is incredibly strong.

Prayer has been documented as a life changing force in times of difficulty. It is an "on behalf of" activity. Creative acts such as dancing and singing materialize prayer in a tangible, kinesthetic way that shifts everyone. Victims see that they are not alone. They often express palpable relief when they see people dance, sing, take up their concerns, move, and pray them up to God.

I wonder if dance might not be one of the most potent forms of intercessory prayer. In a dance and healing group that met for a year, every month we unexpectedly watched our members face the dying of a loved one. We had not realized this would be a theme. As we danced on behalf of those who were dying, we noticed an odd thing. Soon after, the death came quickly and easily, sometimes at the very time the group met. We started joking about our ability to expedite death and help people cross over. Did our danced prayers tangibly effect the physical web of life?

People have an incredible capacity to empathize with each other's troubles. Removing the need for words allows us to communicate and extend that empathy on a more basic, and often more profound level. In dance, as in any service or healing activity, we discover new energy and joy in working on behalf of those in need. In fact, it's easier for most people to dance on behalf of others than to dance for themselves.

PLAY: DANCE ON BEHALF OF: "ON BEHALF OF,"
***LIKE BREATHING*, #14**

Patricia Plude and Amar Khalsa intentionally improvised "On Behalf of" as a prayer. Use it to dance for someone or something you care about. Lift your concern out of your body and into space. You needn't try to heal them. Just dance for them. If this doesn't feel satisfying, do it with a partner. Community can be a crucial element in dancing on behalf of others.

We are not meant to carry or personally transform the burdens of others. This requires too much energy. Bringing our concern out into the active play of the Great Body helps move and change the concern. In creative play, anything can happen: humour, vision, answers. We are not required to suffer in the dance or come up with answers. Just dance. Best of all, the dancing we do on behalf of others works on our behalf as well. Things that need healing or health in us rearrange themselves in surprising ways.

Both wounding and healing are communal events. Even when we are hurt by just one person, we heal more quickly if our communities stand with us afterward. I remember a woman who brought her family's mental illness to the dancing community. I asked anyone who had family experience with mental illness if they would like to dance on behalf of her family. Ten people stood up. She found herself suddenly and surprisingly surrounded by those who knew the hardship of family mental illness. Their dance liberated some of the shame she held. She saw and felt the collective sorrow and compassion for mental illness as it was kinesthetically lifted up. Lightening her burden helped her and her family.

Gay people know too well the heart wrenching difficulty of communal alienation. Family and religion are often their harshest judges. Absorbing the judgments of the group and thereby embodying communal disapproval, it is not until families and religious groups stand and speak with pride on their behalf that gay people feel greater ease. Dancing on behalf of the full affirmation of gay people goes beyond word into action, where real healing occurs. When every cell of our being sings and dances a "Yes" to sexual diversity, we affirm life in a hugely transformative way.

Most of us have more on our plate than we are meant to carry: money, work, family, cultural hate or anxiety, illness, wounds. In community, a dance on your behalf, or on behalf of someone you suffer with, can occur by offering little more than a word. Others don't need the whole story. Part of the beauty of dance is that it meets us below the specific details, at the place of universal experience and energy.

PLAY: CREATE FOR ONE ANOTHER

In a group of three people, one person will improvisationally dance or sing on behalf of one of the other two. The third person will witness and be present to the one whose concerns are being lifted up. When you dance or sing, remember to let this also be for you. You needn't heal the person. Only lift up their concern, for their benefit and for your own. As you end the dance, take time to be still, and to rest in the dance before checking in or processing. When you have had some time to reflect together, shake your body out a little, take some deep breaths, and use your easy focus so as not to get too tense or too full. You may want to do this process again, giving each person a chance to experience a dance or song done on their behalf.

———

Masankho Banda tells of going to a juvenile detention centre to work with a group of boys. When he entered the room, they slouched in their chairs in a circle and looked at him askance. They were resistant, showing no interest in having anything to do with him.

"Can you think of something good that someone has done for you?" Masankho asked.

"Ha! Are you kidding?" one kid retorted incredulously, "No one ever did anything good for me."

"No one ever sang you a song?" Masankho asked.

The boys laughed, as if Masankho had just said the stupidest thing in the world.

"No, no one," said the kid.

Masankho acted quickly. "Well, I am going to sing you a song, right now, a song that I am making just for you. It is your song."

The kids' eyes opened. The room grew still. Masankho asked the boy his name and then began to sing to him a song made up in that moment. Tears fell from the young man's stunned eyes. When the song ended, there was not a dry eye in the room. Each boy wanted a song sung on his behalf. They would not let Masankho go until he had sung to every boy in the circle.

Dancing or singing on behalf of others heightens our intolerance for inhuman circumstances and builds desire to find solutions. Like treasure in a field, each person becomes an indispensable gift in the group body. We invest our spirit in them. If we refuse to dance with any person, we refuse treasure for ourselves. Lift up each person's life and needs as treasure, and the whole city begins to glitter. A folk song that Masankho taught me says it well.

> I'm going to lift my brother up, he's not heavy.
> I'm going to lift my sister up, she's not heavy.
> I'm going to lift my people up, they're not heavy.
> If I don't lift them up.
> If I don't lift them up.
> If I don't lift them up.
> I will fall down.

When you sing and dance and dream with them, people are not too heavy for us.

———

"THAT SONG AND DANCE HAD THE POWER
TO PERFORM MIRACLES."

BARBARA LEVENBROOK

Barbara Levenbrook's friend Mary Ann had central nervous system
lupus, a disease that kept her housebound and in pain.
Eight InterPlayers made a difference on a Sunday afternoon when
they came to dance, sing, and play for her and the family dog,
Peabody. This is Barbara's thank-you letter to the group
Off the Deep End.

I am so deeply moved, I don't think I can express it even now. I am moved, first, by the generosity of the eight players (and their fortitude in 92-degree heat with intermittent jet noises, not to mention Peabody's attentions at the beginning). I was particularly moved by the beautiful and strong counterbalancing dance of Tom and Bob on hope and pain. Mary Ann was moved by that as well, and said it reminded her of Pilobolus, which is her favourite dance group. She remarked, when you were warming up, that everyone was "so comfortable in their bodies," and then sighed and said, "I wish I could do that."

I especially appreciated, as well, the hand dance the group did on stage (and that you invited us to do) to Curran Reichert's "If I Take the Wings of the Morning." As you know, this song is a loose translation of Mary Ann's favourite psalm. That was a song and dance that had the power to perform miracles. I have watched Mary Ann's stamina and energy deteriorate for six years now. Just before that piece, she whispered to me, "Barb, I'm fading fast," and closed her eyes. Normally, that means she will zonk out and have to be led/carried back to bed. However, something you did just before that piece made her snap her eyes open, and she sat upright, and was alert for at least three more hours thereafter. I haven't seen that amount of energy in her in three years. She tried to do the hand dance, thought better of it, tried to take your invitation to close her eyes and imagine dancing, but the pull of the bodies on the "stage" was too great. She opened her eyes, and they filled with grateful tears, as she watched you all. I saw her face relax and glow.

You noticed, I hope, that she also laughed a lot, guffawing from the gut, and every time she did so, I saw her gain energy. Her colour, which was pasty at first (a sign of physical strain in her) improved as you continued. We both really liked Donna's three-sentence story blurt on mosquitoes, but Mary Ann put it best: "I will never look at mosquitoes the same way again." And she smiled, as I did, when Janet calmly explained, "Cats are equal to God. Dogs are not."

Afterward, as she sat in her bed, I found her chatting animatedly with Judith, and I don't know who else. When I came into the bedroom, she said, "I will live off that for six months." Mistakenly thinking she was talking about the food, I pointed out there weren't that many leftovers. She corrected me: "I mean the energy. There was lots of it, and it was all positive."

I could go on and on about the things I enjoyed (like Tom's story-song about big trees), but I want to return to the effects on Mary Ann one more time. I really do think that you accomplished miracles yesterday. Normally, for Mary Ann to exert herself to dress, and sit up and interact with other adults outside of her bed, she must pay a price: extra pain for days thereafter. We both expected this reaction, but it hasn't happened. I saw her again today. She was sitting up in bed, alert and refreshed. She said, wonderingly, "You know, the reaction hasn't been bad yet today." I told her, in my best Merlin manner, that it wouldn't be. She protested: "But I used up so much energy yesterday." I replied, "But you took in so much more."

God bless all you miracle workers and dear friends,
Barbara

24

FREE TIME
GOING THE SPEED
OF THE BODY

In 1997 I broke down. My body stopped, my energy dropped out, and I couldn't stop crying. All I could carry was myself and that felt too hard. I was frightened and disabled by this dramatic change in myself. I immediately went to the doctor and was diagnosed with a mild form of depression, dysthymia. It was an odd thing for vibrant, irrepressible, playful me. Accused of being over active, of loving and taking on too much, I had been trying to balance my energy for years while bouncing between being ecstatically outgoing and exhausted in any given day. Turning 40, my increasing family responsibilities, financial challenges, and peri-menopausal metabolic changes – they all took a toll.

My body demanded a slow-down. So I took out my contact lenses, let air and light kiss my eyeballs, sat my leaden body down in the backyard, watched the slow greening of spring, took deep breaths, and decided to let nature heal me. Instead of trying to get back up to speed and using all the coping mechanisms I had developed over the years, I attempted an experiment. I decided to let my mental illness be cured by rest, the earth, and drugs. I chose not to "will" myself better, but to wait upon my health, like a pregnant mother waiting for a baby to be born.

Within days of this decision, the infamous, unfillable hole that is a trademark of depression, opened up in my chest. It shocked me. Even then I committed to not working myself up. In the following months, the wisdom of the earth broke through. I began to have visions of the tree of life. Lying on the floor doing deep breathing, eyes closed, I had a vision that I was at the foot of a tremendous world-sized tree, its branches teeming with life, the magnificent tree of life spoken of in Genesis and the Book of Revelation, the biblical beginning and end of time. Afterward, I began seeing the tree of life everywhere I looked. I found it in Native American traditions, Buddhism, Celtic religion, Judaism's Kabbalah, Sufism, Shaker spirituality, the Enneagram, and Goddess religions.

Next, I realized that humans are like trees: trunk and limb, bronchial forests populating our lungs, fed by placentas that leave a tree print when pressed onto paper, our nervous system branching off from the spinal column into fine limbs and feathery twigs. "Tree of Life" is the translation for Latin anatomical names for locations in the brain and female reproductive system. Our roots, fruits, and family tree are all a part of our embodied self-image.

My bodyspirit was rearranging itself to a natural structure instead of a mechanistic one. The tree was given as a more sustainable architecture for living. Ideology, theology, and progress, all somehow associated with the brain, give us systems, but too often ask for more than a body can deliver. Now, instead of viewing my brain as centre, the living tree of my spine was becoming centre.

In a dream, I gave birth to a brand new backbone. Having backbone and standing up for my own needs were no longer metaphors. Becoming a dancing tree, I felt myself as earth stuff. I was relearning how to sit on old stumps and how to follow different energetic impulses. Then, one day, inside the lightning burned-out inside of an old redwood in the Santa Cruz mountains, I spontaneously covenanted with the tree to help and be helped by the Tree of Life and all trees.

Creativity, health, body, spirit, and earth life are no longer side-burner issues. Urban life is intense. Pushed to stay up, go, go go, produce, produce, produce, many of us break down. Responsibilities multiply and exhaust us and we feel ashamed by our inability to keep up. Romantic hearts, searching minds, and dauntless spirits lead the way. The body? Everything seems to demand that we rise above our animal bodies. Adopting values of hard work and self-sacrifice, we allow ourselves to be treated as replaceable components in a productivity machine. But, ultimately, human bodies don't work as programmable cogs. Being laid off or run into the ground robs our life. Institutions that over-shape or overrun us hurt us more than serve us.

Bodies don't lie. Failing to go the speed of our body and the speed of the earth body, our generations are showing the cost. A recent study called the "Times Value Survey" focussed on attitudes toward time and reported that of the interviewees

- 31 percent felt constantly under stress;
- 31 percent worry that they don't spend enough time with family and friends,
- 27 percent feel trapped by daily routine, and
- 61 percent would be "willing to forgo 20 to 40 percent of their income for a day or two of free time each week.

The first instinct of many adults and children today is to lie down, hide out, or just get away. We need unstructured body time. We need free time to have free bodies. We need to move at the speed of the body. How fast is that? For some, it is much slower. For others, it is wilder and more dynamic than sitting at a desk allows.

———

MEDITATION: "OFFERING,"
LIKE BREATHING, #15
Nancy Brink's poem speaks to how slowly life must be poured – like an offering, as if this moment is all that matters.

———

PRACTICE AND JOURNAL: THE SPEED OF YOUR BODY
Look out your window. Take a deep breath. Go for a walk in a natural place. Sit in the garden. Observe the world in motion. How fast does it seem to you? What is your speed? Is it in line with the natural world? Is your energy sustainable? Can you let the speed of the earth-dance hold you and be there for you?

———

"Mommy, what would happen if the earth stopped going around?" six-year-old Katie asked me. Caught totally off guard, I gasped a little and then calmly said, "I don't know. I guess things would get really hot on one side and really cold on the other and...and everything would die."

Katie's question broke through my forgetfulness. The earth turns. Earth and all the other planets whirl through the solar system...dancing. Etymologically, the word "universe" means "turning of the one." All heavenly bodies, stars, solar systems, and all that lives in the universe, dances on my behalf with very little help from me.

———

PRACTICE AND JOURNAL: LET EARTH DO THE TURNING

Let earth do the turning for a moment. Do you want to sit or lie down? Do you want to sing or dance for joy? What if you could go the speed of your body more often? Would you enjoy life more? Would you be willing to live more simply in order to have a life that is more easy-going?

———

Some days earth is the only one left who can dance. We go to nature for this very reason, to reconnect with the unconditional beauty of life. Earth does not require mechanistic unison or full-on productivity to make things happen. One isn't required to do the exact steps or go the same direction as others. To the contrary, going the speed of the body is how earth best sustains life.

Ellen Oak found it hard to find grace while living out of hectic, cerebral forms of modern community. She found herself always asking,

How can I be most helpful? Most useful? What's the best use of my gifts and talents? So burdened by what should I do? What is the Right Thing To Do? The Good Thing? The Best Thing? These questions brought me years of anxiety and sorrow. There is no way to figure this out in a rational manner. I spent years feeling pressured by the burden of my talents, so afraid I would not Make The Most of What I Have, not Live Up to My Potential, and that I would have to answer for my laziness and fear before someone, some judge, God, my father, the angels in heaven?

In the last five years, putting quality of life ahead of career advancement; returning to the part of earth that feels like my flesh, like I am made of this earth, I belong here; discovering and settling into a primary relationship of joy, respect, freedom, honesty, and consistent, committed, mutual presence; hitting middle-age – I have let go of trying to answer that question from the outside in and have turned my attention to listening closely to my own bodyself, and let emerge what emerges, however small and fragile and formless it looks to me. This is enough. Enough goodness. It is enough.

Alan Watts once said,

How long have the planets been circling the sun? Are they getting anywhere and do they go faster and faster in order to arrive? How often has the spring returned to the earth? Does it come faster and faster every year, to be sure to be better than the last spring, and hurry on its way to the spring that shall out spring all springs?

Undone by the majestic movement of the heavens, those who get true glimpses of our universe regularly fall to their knees. Lying down on the earth, letting earth move us for a while is not something of which to be ashamed. The body moves in a grace much wiser than that of a busy mind. Most religions teach a simpler way, a way that pays strict attention to the physics of love, respect, and our unity with all things. We need to do more than believe in this wisdom. We must practice it.

———

PRACTICE AND JOURNAL: THE DANCE OF INCREMENTALITY
Take a walk around your room or out of doors. Taking time, intentionally and simply put one foot in front of the other. Look for a destination nearby and walk toward it. Find an easy way to be present to each step. You may need to walk slower or faster. Stop anytime you like and rest. Now choose another destination. This time take a circuitous, wandering path. Occasionally take a big step or even a leap for fun. Embodied results happen step by step. Can you stay with your body each step of the way? Making the steps as much fun as you can makes life a dance.

———

Though I was raised in the vast metropolis of Los Angeles, my father was an outdoorsman who took us out into the wild one weekend each month. Windy bluffs and sandy gullies, granite outcroppings and pine forests drew songs and dreams from me. I played house with sticks and rocks, climbed to the top of desert buttes, sang love songs to the sea, and made forts out of piles of grass, until college, career, marriage, and inward adventures gradually distanced me from the wilderness. Reintegrating a regular earth practice into my urban life was a challenge. Was my distance from nature contributing to my lack of wisdom about the speed of the body? The Tree of Life seem to be saying, "Yes, get thee to a tree."

So I began gathering people to walk together once a month into a nearby state park where there was a redwood and bay grove. I needed a group to keep me accountable to going, I am sad to say. In this grove, I began to play and pray in the oldest sanctuary around. My practice continues. With others, I walk in silence into Redwood Regional Park, acutely sensing seasonal changes, temperatures, moisture, colour, and smells. I feel myself slow down. Sighs come. I remember the speed of this body, the body in nature. We cross a footbridge over a stream bed and arrive at a three-row amphitheatre surrounded by arcs and spears of bay trees that screech and sing with the breezes. After ten or 15 minutes, we honour the earth by making offerings of movement, songs, prayers, shrines, and stories. Sometimes we ask her to speak through us.

Teaching and dancing in the forest is different than any other dance I do. I am less formed in my approach, less programmatic. The beauty of the place is enough. Little is needed except respect. Asking so little and offering so much, the trees and grass and canyon are now sacred to me. A relationship has formed that is not just personal. It is communal. The grove lives in my body. I belong to it. Its story and the stories of my community intertwine in the life of human, tree, animal, bird, rock, air, water, and weather.

Some say we must start to think more like our planet in order to survive these times. It might be easier and faster if we just start dancing with earth, first. The fastest way to inspire change is through relationship and the faster way to build relationship is to dance and share a story with someone. Slowing down to do the earth dance and going the speed of the body will nourish and bring peace, beauty, and strength now.

"I WOULD NOT BE DESCRIBED AS LAZY.
WOULD THAT I WERE!"

———

MARY FOY

a senior Sister of Mercy from New Zealand,
joined the Sophia Center class in Oakland, California,
in the redwoods, and danced into earth mysticism.

I did some flying among the trees today and it was great fun!
My kite (a hand dance) took me soaring among the birds, above
the trees, and into another place. I enjoyed that. I like to free
flow, but I would not be described as lazy. Would that I were!

What we are doing as we spend time in Redwood Park is
about body, nature, and place. This is a growing experience as I
move from a dualistic paradigm that separates body from mind,
and human from other species. Over the weeks, I am more
deeply aware of the communities of life in the forest – those
under my feet, those above my head, and those in front of me
and all around me. Today, a furry rodent joined us. I rejoice
that she felt so comfortable in her home and was able to stay
close by and keep on with her tasks. Later, when I crossed the
open space to return to the group, the birds knew that this is
their place. They did not need to fly away, but rather continued
their gathering before flying off at sunset.

Particularly significant today was a deep awareness that as I
wander through the park I am *manuhiri*, a visitor. As I spent
time in the first grove of redwoods, aware of the communities
of that grove, I realized in a different way that my relationship
with the living communities of this bioregion is very like my
relationship with Mauri and other Pacific Island people at home.

I enter their *marae* with reverence and respect, and only with an invitation, on their terms. Mauri and Pacific Island people have formal welcoming ceremonies. When I am welcomed onto the *marae* with *powhiri*, the protocol of welcome, I am then accepted as *tangata whenua*, people of the land, and join in welcoming further guests. Today I became aware that being in nature requires a similar reverence and respect.

Over the weeks as we have walked and spent time among the redwoods and their forest community, I have realized that while I have spent a huge amount of my time in the Waitakere and Coromandel Ranges since childhood, and have tramped three- to four-day tracks among other mountains, this experience is different. Previously I have been going somewhere – to the end of the track six or seven or ten hours later! This is about presence, awareness, relationship, interconnectedness. What I already know about reverence in another's place, on another's *whenua*/land, I am applying to being in creation. This is a paradigm shift for me.

I better understand what Rangi Davis, Kaiarataki, and Te Tairere Oranga, explained to me about the heart of Maoritanga in the concept of *tapu*. *Tapu* is the inner essence of all things; it rises from the mauri or life-force. Encounters of *tapu* with *tapu*, of one being with another, involve restrictions on people and objects, on places, and events. *Tapu* requires care and discernment in how we handle objects, in how we treat our environment and the world that sustains us. Tapu is what keeps all creation safe.

I intend to continue this spiritual practice when I return home. We often gather for sunset as a spiritual practice on a mountain above our home among low-income families. The kids often join us, so there are opportunities already there.

DANCING LIFE'S DIFFICULT DANCES

25

DANCING LIFE'S DIFFICULT DANCES

These last stories are exercises in themselves, exercises in believing that we can have a profound, creative, physical relationship to any circumstance: death, aging, the loss of a child, imprisonment, our own death, even war. Sheila Collins, Don Moseman, Krista Harris, Peggy King, Beth Hoch, and Ginger Trang Le are testaments to grace, to InterPlay, and to soulful living. They know what the body wants and they've been to the place in that old spiritual *Rock-a My Soul* that is, "so deep you can't get under it, so wide you can't get around it, so high you can't get over it. You've got to go through the door." They have walked through the door of life in all of its awful glory – and they dance.

To do the difficult dances of life with powerful ease it is best that we start dancing, breathing, singing, and playing before the hard times come. We need to take a deep breath NOW and remember that the world is in motion.

Open to the physicality of grace right where you are. That

is the biggest leap. You can do it sitting in a chair. It won't kill you, but everything will feel at stake. You are likely to become bigger, more visionary, and to gain more clarity about what is important. You are likely to have more fun. When this happens, miracles occur. Jean Houston, in her book *Godseed: The Journey of Christ,* says

when we cease seeking grace and let it find us; we become grace. And thus nature becomes grace, people become grace, the cosmos becomes grace. Ah, the joy being brought down to earth, for down is up in the mystic world. The souls of mystic pilgrims are the soles of their feet, where they touch the ground of being; it is the image and the likeness of God. From past to present it has been our feet that connected us to the Ultimate. The mystic dance is done in two-step – left and right, yin and yang, to and from, up and down.

In what feels like a challenging time in history, a time when we speak of saving the earth, ending war, and finding love beyond borders, some of us will have to dance more and talk less. Policies are not enough. The mind is not enough. The spirit is not enough. Our whole being needs to feel integrated to create quality of life and relationship. Our embodiment – imaginative and unstoppably resourceful – is key.

DANCE OF AGING AND LOSS

SHEILA COLLINS

danced to survive and transform aging, professional losses,
and her son's death to AIDS.

Dance has always gotten me through. Even my kids noticed. "Mom, it's time for you to go dancing," they would say when I got out of sorts with them. And it would work. After a dance class, I'd return relaxed, invigorated, and so very glad to see my children. Meanwhile, my mother-in-law thought it was awful that I left those children with a sitter to go dancing.

Now I'm an old person and I still dance (and still get out of sorts when I don't). I have continued to use dance for my own self-care, and through InterPlay have added storytelling and vocalization to exform and transform my life experience. I often say to myself, especially about dancing, "How long can you realistically keep this up? You are (I fill in the age I happen to be at the time), so you are living on borrowed time." I now tease myself that I have entered the "extra point category," in the way that gymnastic or diving moves are graded upwards for degree of difficulty. At 62, I am taking every opportunity I can to dance and perform and teach, because I find it the most remarkable tool for authentic, joyful living.

I was a professional dancer. I did summer stock, industrial shows, supper clubs, was in the national company of a Broadway show, and in a dance scene of a now classic movie that is shown on television nearly every year. When my husband's job took us away from New York, I could no longer make a living as a dancer or performing artist. I had children and tried to deal with the tremendous loss I felt at not having a profession, at not having a good excuse to dance and perform.

I started back to school taking a couple of classes a semester, not daring to think about how long it would take or what I would do when I finished. On campus, I ran into Harriet Berg, who directed a semi-professional modern dance company out of the Jewish Community Center in Detroit. She had been commissioned to choreograph Leonard Bernstein's *Chichester Psalms* and asked me to join her company, Festival Dancers. We danced in churches and synagogues, on marble floors in museums, on cement patios at street fairs, and on the grassy knolls of county fairs (we toured the upper peninsula of Michigan in a van). And sometimes we even danced in theatres.

It was during the six years I was with the Festival Dancers that I began to understand some of what was so wonderful about dancing. Once, we were performing in a church at the same time as one of our company members was travelling in a Middle-Eastern country. The news media reported that hostilities had broken out there. Company members joined together in a prayer before the service. Performing on her behalf for her safety, I got to the point where I became the dance, and I experienced the dance dancing me.

The body memory of the dance dancing me has been a spiritual touchstone in my life. I got the idea that if I could experience life as a dance, life could feel graceful, rhythmical, and blessedly full. As a professional social worker and therapist, I used the metaphor of dance with students and clients and even used it as the central theme in my book *Stillpoint: The Dance of Selfcaring, Selfhealing*, about self-care for caregivers.

Finding InterPlay has brought together all the threads of my experiences, of my efforts for healing, health, and holiness. And the community that is created when people come together to play – this has satisfied a deep need in me to lighten up and to not take myself or anything too seriously.

Dance has helped me make it through extremely difficult times. For over ten years, I've belonged to a women's spirituality group that meets four weekends a year. Once a season, we leave our regular lives and go to the woods, to the lake, or to a ranch – to sing and dance, and to tell our stories to one another. We often construct an altar where we put pictures of family members we are praying for, or objects that represent some aspect of our lives that we wish to transform. One particular winter I brought a CD of the Glide Memorial Choir and I decided to dance to their version of the spiritual "God Is Good to Me!" Before the proceedings began, I had placed a picture of my son, Kenneth, on the altar. He was in his late 20s at the time and living with AIDS. I began to dance to the song, "Sometimes in this life when things are tough," and "I haven't been as good as I should be – yet, God is good to me." As the song progressed and that spirit-filled choir began to pick up steam, "come what may, let it be" – from all the multiple objects on the altar, Ken's picture caught my eye. Without thinking, I grabbed the picture in its frame to my bosom, and continued dancing. "God stepped in, right on time," the song continued to an emotional crescendo, "God is good to me!"

It has been years now since my son's death, but as I write about that experience, I re-experience the joy that flowed through my body that day during that transformational dance. When I first learned of Ken's diagnosis, I was given the advice I would have given one of my clients: "Find a way to say yes to what you cannot change." The dance I did that day took me to the place of "Yes." The bodyspirit memory of that dance sustained me through the next three-year journey of accompanying my son as he lived and died with AIDS. A friend, who was a witness on that occasion, told me later, "Yes! Yes! That's it! In the Sufi tradition, the teaching is to pick up whatever life has given you and dance with it!"

The older I get, the more unlikely a dancer I become. The goal to "keep dancing" has had a big impact on my life, on the way I take care of myself, on the way I am aging. In some groups that I am involved with, I'm probably considered an old person who doesn't act her age. In the InterPlay community, I am an elder with interesting stories to dance and sing. I've even been called a "fairy grandmother!" Surely it can't get much better than that!

INTERPLAYING A NEW LIFE SENTENCE

DON MOSEMAN

"Walking Don" spent most of his life in San Quentin State Penitentiary. Leaving prison he had to learn how to live, love, move around, and be human, as if from scratch.

I spent my first five years in a foster home. My mother couldn't take care of me, so right out of the nursery at San Francisco General Hospital in 1939, the end of the depression, I was given up. The foster home locked me in a closet at that time. That's why I love being outside. My grandfather and grandmother found out bad things were happening to me so they got me back when I was five years old. Even today I have this incredible fear of confinement.

Growing up in San Francisco as a little boy was so exciting. There were so many things happening at once. The PG&E power plant at the end of 22nd Street was my play spot, about two miles from my grandparent's house. There was this cement canal with water gushing through it into a tunnel that went into the bay. I was fascinated by the water, but already knew not to fall in for I could be swept away. One day I was leaning over the railing watching the water and feeling the warmth of the sun when all of a sudden I felt as though someone was there. I turned and saw a tall man in a dark suit with the sky so blue behind him. He had a neatly trimmed beard but what I really noticed were his eyes. They were so gentle and kind. I had no fear of him. My grandfather stuck out his hand towards me and I put my hand in his and he took me home.

My grandfather protected me and wouldn't let anyone harm me, but he soon died and then everything changed. All of a sudden my mother was in the house and then I was always getting beat up, for they couldn't keep me in school or the house.

The day came that my mother took me to juvenile hall for wandering. Two things happened to me: one, I hated being locked up; and two, I accepted it because my mother put me in. So I would escape when I could, but the system would lock me deeper and deeper. When I got so I could steal cars, the police always ended up in a wild chase. So my life was spent in the youth authority. When I turned 18, I was sent to San Quentin. I was in and out of prison until 1989. I've had seven prison commitments and a history of heroin addiction. It didn't look like I would quit.

The system was sick and tired of me. I just kept coming back. The last time I had been out four months and into my heroin addiction full blown when I got a telegram from the parole people. It said, "Come to the office now. Don't phone or go to a job." I don't know why I went down, but I did. They sat me down and said, "Straighten out or you're going to prison for the rest of your natural life." They finally got my attention. In 1989, the doors of San Quentin opened for me for the last time. Been good ever since. Found out if I don't break the law, I won't go to jail – so easy. But I also found out that life is hard and this is where my journey began.

My world in jail had no movement so I had to learn how to move in the world. I didn't know how to be accountable and responsible. All these things people out here know and seem to do so easily – like work, pay bills, play – that's what I wanted to do. I had been so deprived of playing and so hard on myself. I needed to learn how to be gentle with myself.

One day I met Susan and Julie. They both belonged to InterPlay. I used to tell them "You'd only catch me dead dancing." I got this flyer in the mail from them inviting me to a retreat. So I went – ten women and me. The next morning, after we ate, we all went to the dance floor and did something called walk, stop, run. I could do that. But then the solos came. Two gals got up and danced. I never saw anything like that. Well it was my turn. They said, "Go." And I said, "No." They said, "Just get up there." So I did. I didn't know what I was supposed to do. They said, just find something that you like to do and move. The only thing I could think of was a deer caught in headlights. So I closed my eyes and just started moving like I thought a deer would move and made it through and finished the retreat.

That was how I got dancing. I kept up the InterPlay classes. I could feel myself stretching. What I was really looking for was to be free. InterPlay was teaching me to stay in the moment, how to pause, find stillness, and most of all, be all right with who I am. I love the physical contact for it is teaching me how to bring in, instead of push away. I practice all the stuff I learn in class and it works so well in everyday life.

Now I trim trees to make money, but what I really love is walking long distances. In 1998, I walked across America. My dreams are coming true.

DANCING AND DYING

KRISTA GEMMELL HARRIS AND PEGGY KING

Krista and Peggy and their community used InterPlay
to grieve, to care for one another, and ultimately
to encounter and pass through death.

In May of 2000, InterPlayers from Seattle, the San Francisco Bay area, and all over the United States gathered for four days of celebration and performances called The Unbelievable Beauty of Being Human. During the Friday evening performance, Peggy King seized the moment to exorcise an old performance demon that had been haunting her for 25 years. From the wings, she thrust her bodyspirit on stage and joined Cynthia Winton-Henry and another female dancer; they were ready to throw themselves into the moment of creation. While four InterPlay singers created an outrageous song about a horse with braces, Peggy unabashedly bared her big teeth, and danced with zany, yet skillful, abandon. Vibrantly alive, claiming her fullness as a dancer and a comedian, Peggy nearly stopped the show with her athleticism, her daring, and her humour. She co-created a delightful ensemble piece with the other two dancers while simultaneously claiming her right to perform and to be fully herself.

Three weeks later, Peggy discovered that she had incurable liver cancer. It was inconceivable that the most athletic and physically vibrant member of Seattle's InterPlay community could have such a profoundly threatening disease. Peggy was the healthiest person we knew. As the weeks and months un-

folded, Peggy and her beloved friends and family members continued to wrestle with this paradox. Peggy was a direct, tell-it-
like-it-is kind of gal. She shared her devastating prognosis with
her InterPlay family as soon as she had the information. A physical therapist, Peggy could share medical information in a calm
and centred way. She always hoped she would be one of the
miracle cures described in the *New England Journal of Medicine*,
but she courageously honoured the very real possibility that
she could die within the year.

Peggy had been a part of an ongoing InterPlay group that
had been meeting on Friday mornings for five years. Close-knit,
we played hard, laughed and cried, learned to be silly with ease,
and encouraged each other to take risks. We knew how to support each other. We had the history of Leah's brain hemorrhage,
Susan and Ingrid's hysterectomies, Peggy's hernia operation,
Marianne's brain tumor, and, earlier, her husband's. Even so,
Peggy's illness stunned us. Our beloved group members had
survived their health challenges; the odds had been in their favour. Not so with Peggy.

I made a personal pledge to Peggy to create a space where
she could dance and sing and tell big body stories about her
journey with cancer as long as she wished. She took me up on
that offer and during the next seven months, various members
of the InterPlay community met 16 times as Peggy's InterPlay
support group. As the leader of this group, I never knew what
to expect and had no certainty about what to do. I just knew
that I needed to show up and hold a container where anything
could happen. My years of experience with InterPlay helped
me have the courage to do this: to be in the moment, to listen
to those intuitive hunches, to risk following through on them,
to be a compassionate witness, to refrain from trying to fix anything, to hang out in stillness, and to ask for help.

Contrary to my expectations, our group never laughed as

hard as it did during our first session with Peggy on July 7. Peggy had been through a series of excruciating medical tests, including a barium enema. The procedures had been administered by unsympathetic technicians who had neglected to explain what they were doing and what physical sensations Peggy might experience. Peggy was furious. She assigned two fellow playmates to play the parts of "Doctors S & M" and the three of them proceeded to relive the painful and violating procedures in a wickedly funny improvised farce. Peggy had a rubber face that could make incredibly funny expressions or break out into a radiant smile. She was a gifted imp with a flair for irreverence. She could twist her voice into demonic textures and tones. Laughing until we wept, this merry and frightened band helped Peggy release her frustrations and fears, her anger and her sense of isolation. We were there for her.

That was our main gift to Peggy. We were there for her. As she gratefully told us one day, we provided the one place in her life where she could express absolutely anything she felt without having to protect the listener. In return, she taught us how to live full-heartedly with living and dying.

Our group was profoundly blessed to have a shared knowledge of InterPlay forms before Peggy's diagnosis. The forms were old friends that helped ground us as our hearts overflowed with feelings. Our previous experiences as witnesses in "solo-witness dances" helped us create a refuge for Peggy, where anything she said or did would be unconditionally accepted. Peggy's familiarity with the forms gave her a variety of ways to creatively share her joys and sorrows. Storytelling is a big part of InterPlay; Peggy told us many a story using words, movement, and hilarious sound effects. Some days, she would belt out her feelings in a fake aria. She usually danced when she needed to express mysterious questions that had no answers. What happens when you die? Why is this happening to me? How can I bear to leave my children? Where is the spiritual gift in all of this?

As our times together continued, Peggy took charge more and more. Her physical vitality was weakening, but her sense of inner authority grew stronger and stronger. Time was running out. She asked for what she wanted. She requested specific InterPlay forms. She also created new forms. Peggy invited people to lead blessings and prayers, to do healing dances, to sit together and meditate. She asked individual people to embody different parts of her emotional body – her fear, her anger, her pain, her sadness. While people danced these feelings, Peggy directed others to embody her physical and spiritual resilience and ecstatically dance among them. She might send an imp in to stir things up. Peggy called for contact dances that paired love with fear, love with anger, love with pain, love with sadness.

Peggy came from a large family. During the course of her illness, all of her family came to visit Peggy and danced and sang with Peggy and our group. I remember one day when Peggy's parents and two of her sisters were with us. Near the end of our gathering, I invited the King family members to do a shape and stillness dance while the rest of us made a big circle around them. George and Betty and their three daughters lovingly played with each other, interweaving arms and legs, hearts and livers, heads and toes. Deep longings for connection and healing within everyone's families of origin were met in that dance. The Kings and their love danced on behalf of all of us.

The first time Peggy took an InterPlay class with me she was seven months pregnant with her cherished son, Gene. Peggy radiated such beauty as she danced with that big belly of boy. Seven years later, her belly had filled out again, only this time Peggy was pregnant with death. Her swollen belly created a haunting contrast against her skeletal form, yet Peggy continued to radiate more and more beauty as time passed.

On our last gathering together, Peggy was very weak and needed long periods of rest. We knew she was too fragile to dance, but she insisted on getting up and dancing nonetheless. As had happened many times before, Peggy came to life in a much bigger way than her body could actually support. She spoke one last time of her profound love and gratitude for all of us. She confessed that she still could not make sense or meaning out of her dying, but that her spirit and her capacity to love had expanded exponentially. With considerable difficulty, Peggy lowered herself to the floor and curled into a tiny ball, symbolizing the place she had been before her diagnosis of cancer. Peggy gently released the tight ball of her body and, with miraculous ease, slowly rose to her feet. Standing tall, her arms and chest opened as she gratefully claimed the expansion of her spirit.

As several tiny tears flowed down her cheeks, Peggy shared her profound sadness about dying. Embodied grief. Embodied love. Embodied gratitude. Peggy's energy rose as she described her enormous desire to eat huge portions of her favourite foods without pain. She had recently dreamed that she had pigged out on chocolate cream pie and a platter of pasta and had awakened to discover that her huge belly was gone and her cancer cured. How we longed for that dream to come true, while staying present with the knowing that it couldn't. Throughout her journey, Peggy had become our spiritual teacher. Her final words of advice to us that day were down to earth and full of bodyspirit wisdom: "Enjoy eating!" Peggy challenged us!

My last dance with Peggy was at her home. She was resting on the couch in her living room. The room has glass windows from floor to ceiling facing a wooded area of evergreen trees. I felt I was in a tree house blessed by the grace and wisdom of tree spirits. I sat down with Peggy. She recognized me and asked if we could meditate together. I played Jennifer Berezan's hauntingly beautiful CD *ReTURNING* and sat down with Peggy. For the next 45 minutes, I simply held Peggy's hand and breathed with her. Peggy appeared to be resting peacefully. I felt at ease – blessed, sad, and happy all at once. At times, my hand gently moved hers in a hand dance. Mostly, we experienced quietude in an extended shape and stillness hand meditation. Even though Peggy's body was wasting away, I did not feel I was with a person who was diminished in any way. At one point, I felt our spirits come together in a vibrant contact duet.

Peggy spoke to me several times, expressing love and gratitude for me and her InterPlay family. Her imp even came out to play for a minute or two! I stayed for the duration of the CD, wishing it would never end. I kissed Peggy and left, hoping to see her again, while knowing that this particular way of being together, body to body, might not happen again. I went to my car and sobbed, rejoicing in the amazing times we had had together singing and speaking and dancing our hearts out. My life would be forever changed.

Peggy's memorial was held on Valentine's Day. Dance was featured and people's hearts poured forth in love and myriad artistic forms. Among the eloquent memorials to Peggy was Victoria Millard's poem *The Sacrament of Waiting*, and this excerpt.

I remember her impish face.
She could jump like a frog and kiss her toes.
She cackled and leaped,
cast a circle holy, complete,
turned upside down and pumped her feet
to a subterranean rhythm.

How the core of her molded
with the body of another,
shape shifting, balancing, flowing together.
When she danced, the mystery unfolded.
Dancer, mother, healer, lover,
her heart weighed against a feather
would show itself lighter by any measure.

Now that she's explored all the faces of leaving,
laughed at the fates,
gathered us in,
raged and cried, done her grieving,
who is she now who waits,
spare as bone and barely human?

A leaf released into the wind rising and falling,
playing with chance,
finally resting in the rarest of gifts,
the dancer who's become the dance.

PRISON INTERPLAY

BETH HOCH AND CYNTHIA WINTON-HENRY

Beth Hoch, a social worker, and I had never been inside prison walls.

BETH

So many beautiful women lowering their heads as we walk by – a caste society – a Third-World country in a first-class nation. They glance up at us as we are introduced as "ladies from the church" over and over again, in spite of the fact that we hadn't mentioned being part of any church. I felt like I was expected to pull out my handkerchief and flit my hand about or fan myself. Suddenly, I imagined my breasts huge and heavy on my chest; my waist thick with a small, tight, narrow belt cinching in my pink-on-white floral dress; the little navy blue hat, having been taken on and off a few too many times, sitting flatly on my gray head; my shoes, black lace-up pumps, holding in feet swelling like bread dough left to rise too long.

No, this was a place to be serious. Like the security checkpoint at the airport, this was clearly no place to make a joke. But then, from the mouth of a short, hard-looking dyke comes the question, "What kind of dance can you do with Jesus?"

Cynthia says, "Any kind you like."

The dyke says, "I'd do a slowwwww dance, man. I'd wrap my legs around Jesus…real tight… mmmmmmm. Yeah…a real slow dance."

A comrade is found. Does she see how glad we are that she breaks the spell? She uncinches the belt from my waist and punches down my swollen façade. What sweet relief!

This community of women, mingling in groups, talking small to each other, so small that you cannot tell if they are communicating at all – it must be something they learn, how to talk and make it look like not talking. They could be actors in a film waiting for the action sign to start the real scene.

We are in a circle in the chapel, discussing what kind of class it will be, who might be interested and how we recruit students. A beautiful black woman in her 50s, with a white scarf on her head, looks like God to me: big, full, beautiful, and clear as a bell. She is a Muslim and her name is Omega.

"They need something to de-stress," she says, "like, perfect example, one of the inmates was in the laundry room, ironing her shirts. She let the iron go on for a while and when she picked it up, a big ol' bellow of steam went up to the ceiling. The guard, he said 'What the hell you doing smoking in there!' I put my hand on her arm 'cause I knew she was uptight, and I tell you, it was stiff! Not just hard, stiff! I tried to calm her down, but they just started in. If she could have stopped to realize that she had seven witnesses to the steam, she could have been okay. But, see, she was sooooo stressed. The stress, it just gets worse and worse here. Yeah, we need something to de-stress. Yeah."

CYNTHIA

Weeks later we're teaching in the prison chapel. As prison volunteers, we're told, "Do not reveal personal information, touch, or bring in gifts." Fortunately or unfortunately, that is what we do when we dance, sing, and put it all out there side by side. No one comes to arrest us for all the freedom it takes to be ourselves. Twenty women laugh, dance, lie on the floor, and rise up singing. There never was a lustier group of singers. Next thing, they want to do solos for each other.

Our bodyspirits expand beyond the prison walls. Many have

children far away. We feel our bodies connect to loved ones over great distance and dance on behalf of the children. These women's beauty, bullshitting, silliness, and sorrow beyond words gets to me. Especially Fatima, a middle-aged woman, elegant even in a gray-green uniform. We tell each other brief stories in dance and talk. I watch as her arm lifts. She stirs the air for ten seconds and then suddenly her arm drops with a weight of intolerable impatience. "I was a childcare provider...my boss was an attorney. They loved me, but someone turned me in...no one goes to jail for babysitting they said...but the judge sentenced me to a year...why? For being Iranian? We fled from Iran. But in America my worst nightmare happened...I miss my daughter, husband. This is not me."

Fatima and I play out very different lives. Yet the tense and fragile air between us holds in this moment. We are one. Now I see why Jesus told the disciples to visit the prisoner. The prisoner lives at the physical locations of human retaliation, at the place where life keeps dissolving into death-making. If we lose contact with this place in our culture, we abandon justice and forgiveness.

Side by side, prisoner and free, we are in it together.

I dance with and on behalf of Fatima.

FROM WAR, I DANCE

CECILIA TRANG LE

Cecilia Trang Le and her family escaped Vietnam by boat on their
ninth attempt to leave their homeland. After becoming a U.S.
citizen, working with AIDS children, joining a religious community,
and earning two degrees, she still longed for happiness.

Not too long ago, I knew nothing of peace and too little of
joy. Born during the war in Vietnam, I was fed daily by the
anguishes and fears of my people. For the first 16 years of my
life, my movements were taught to hide; silence was my home
language. Spirit was held hostage and my body carried sorrows
of three generations. I understood nothing of peace.

Now living in the land of "Life, Liberty, and the Pursuit of
Happiness," I have begun to dance my way; to embracing new
life, new freedom; and to entertain myself with possibilities.
Yet the more I dance, the more I remember. I remember how
poverty and war destroy life and the dignity of being. I remember how painful it is to witness my father in chains and beaten
by another human. I remember how fearful it is to live in the
shooting zone, and how hopeless to go to bed each night knowing that I might wake up in the bloodshed of my mother or
sisters.

With memories of war, I am now consciously breathing
for peace, and I dance because I can't afford to forget my ancient connections. I dance to remember who I was and who I
have become. I dance to ask questions that my ancestors couldn't
ask. I dance because tragedies and miracles of life are simply
too much for me to comprehend rationally. I dance to face my
own hatred and to practice self-forgiving. I dance in memory

of, on behalf of, and instead of. Each dance makes visible a new space in me for compassionate relationships. Weaving through memories of violence and grief, I dance to embrace my own limitations and truth. I dance to create new images of my neighbours. I dance to touch the hearts of others who are in every way different than me. I dance to the common language of breathing bodies, to the universal emotions and desires.

And I will continue to be a beginner of dance... I dance at the speed of my body and stay connected to my heart, in order to be truthful. I dance attentively to each joint and bone that holds my body together, in order to learn compassion. I dance celebrating my breathing cells and muscles, in their joys and pains, in order to honour the harmony of our whole earth. Each day I dance a new story, and the Story unfolds a new dance in me. In the community of awakening bodies, our human stories of birthing and dying, of love and fear, of joys and sorrows, of darkness and light, of void and fulfillment, all become one whirling resonance – the Dance of the Eternal Universe.

AFTERWORD

FEAR OF THE BODY

After reading this book, you may wonder how something so basic, magical, and transformative as play, voice, our stories, and dance could become so trivialized. You may have started looking for playmates and still find yourself alone. Where are the playful, grace-creating people? Everyone seems locked in a collective dependence on words, ideas, sitting, and analysis – even those in institutions offering more integrated approaches.

Betsy Wetzig, dance educator, says, "Whenever something loses spiritual necessity, it dies away." The amazing story of how dance and full kinesthetic play – humankind's most beautiful, powerful, and thoroughly embodied spiritual form – came to be so degraded in industrialized society may be the mythic, under-told tale of our time; a story that parallels the splitting of body, indigenous, and feminine wisdom from common life. Though not an historian myself, clues that I have found to this mysterious untold tale lie in the following places:

- in the development of *print and information technology* and the loss of oral and body-to-body communication forms;

- in *cultural conquests* that subsumed and forbade indigenous dancing, drum, and language their previous influence;
- in rampant *immigration* and the loss of traditional practices and body memories;
- in the advance and eventual domination of *reason and science* as a check against abuses wrought by those using subjective practices;
- in the rise of the *work ethic* during the challenging era of the 20th century's industrial nation building;
- in *education's move toward informational instruction* models that demand seated, standardized classroom conduct;
- in *gender role changes* including loss of male dance leadership and feminism's rebellion against female body-centred, emotion-based role typing;
- and in the collective accumulation of *trauma and abuse* from war, economic instability, uprootedness, and family violence, that weighs on our communities, making the vulnerable, uprooted experiences of dance, art, and play counter-intuitive.

In spite of all the stripping and ripping away at the dance of life, it is still here. The dance appears in concert arenas and clubs and anywhere drums play. Youth and adults alike follow global singers past racial and class division, to the place where irrepressible rhythms take hold. It may not be considered spiritual activity, but people who sing and dance know they feel better for doing it.

The courage to dance and play is boosted by the crisis we face today. Rebelling against all the anti-body, anti-creation trends, Emma Goldman said it best: "If I can't dance I don't want to be a part of your revolution!" The urgent need to realign with our planet, to restore cultural and multicultural connection and relationships, and to resurrect our body wisdom from the ashes of neglect and abuse, may foretell that the wants and ways of the body are again a spiritual necessity.

Dancing, singing, telling our story, and playing, propel the unstoppable force of life in human community. Though we may be afraid of looking silly and of humiliating ourselves, it might be worth it. Instead of running to the far corners of the earth looking for something new, the exotic truth is right in our own skin. The leap over fear and self-consciousness into our own body wisdom is not as big as we think. It is so accessible, it stares back at us from the mirror; we are already dancing. In spite of ourselves, we are invited to take one curious step toward grace, to offer just one hand or one deep breath at a time – small acts of faith for incredible inconceivable rewards: joy, ease, fullness of life, and yes, even world peace!

My prayer for us all is to let fear itself help us fall toward the dance of grace and to know little by little that there is nothing so great as this dance. We of the InterPlay community know how hard it is to believe that this can ever happen. Like everyone else, we are stunned that more and more often, we live this dream.

ALISON LUTERMAN

poet and InterPlayer at the Interplayce Grand Opening.

Dreaming, we dreamed our bodies were infinite,
and the spirit in them went on dancing,
finding the necessary other bodies.
We took the first steps out into the starry floor of our
dreams.

Dreaming, we dreamed our bodies were infinite,
and yet we clothed them in fancy pants and dance shoes
and feather boas and glitter,
and we made a house, a dance-house, dream-house,
building it out of vision and word and paper money,
and two-by-fours and strong backs bending to the task,
and broken drill bits, and paint plaster and shellac,
and evil-smelling rubber cement.
We made it out of all these things:
Earth, blood, vision, paper, coffee, phone calls, plane tickets,
love, and music.
Dreaming, I dreamed a house with all my friends,
and all the people I had once called my enemies.
We were dancing together, we were playing with each other.
We were entering and leaving each others' bodies with such
grace,
with such respect,
that the old wounds where we had entered and left without
skill
were healed.
We were not healing our wounds, we were only dancing
and the music was coming through and around us,
from the floorboards to the stars.

GRATITUDE

Martin Luther King, Jr. said, "Occasionally in life there are those moments of unutterable fulfillment which cannot be completely explained by those symbols called words. Their meanings can only be articulated by the inaudible language of the heart."

If whole-hearted gratitude is best expressed in the heart language of dance, then I ask these words to dance, for the overwhelming contributions of so many people make this book an expression of the growing community of InterPlay. You, whose stories live between and within the words and lines of these pages – Phil Porter and I are lifted on your wings. This is your book.

To the gracious power behind, under, and around my life, I bow my deepest bow. You have returned to me my creative fires: dance, word, story, song, stillness, and breath. You continuously help me to remove obstacles of despair and to return to joy. Grace of the Universe, you are my solace and home. In you I move and have my being. Thank you for the genes that tumbled into me through my rollerskate-dancing mom and marathon-running dad. Thank you for revealing yourself in high school through the flashing eyes of Reverend Ray Ragsdale at First Methodist Church, who asked me to choreograph the

Lord's Prayer for worship; and through Mrs. Mac, my high school physical education teacher, who drove me 100 miles on a Saturday to meet Reverend Michael Taxer, the New York City dancer turned Presbyterian minister, and who then steered me toward the UCLA Dance Department. Thank you for leading me to my mentors: Carla deSola, Judith Rock, Doug Adams, Jake Empereur, Barbara Eliot, Flora Wuellner, Pat deJong, Robert McAfee Brown, Betsy Weitzig, Phyllis Magal, and Roberta Meyer.

My work is sustained through my friends: Anne Sigler, you are at the heart of all I do. Thank you for editing and caring for this book along with Pat Pothier. Beth Hoch, Katharine Kunst, Trisha Watts, Rod Pattenden, Steve Harms, Trish Delaney, and Nika Quirk: you are all so good looking. Thank you for holding the vulnerabilites of my vision and giving my chicken wings the power of the eagle.

Wing It! Performance Ensemble, you are our sanctuary and turbo engine of creativity and bodyspirit community: Masankho Banda, Julie Caffey, Suzanne Cimone, Elizabeth Frye, Beth Hoch, Michelle Jordan, Leo Keegan, Amar Khalsa, Cecilia Trang Le, Kirk Livingston, Alison Luterman, Susan Main, Penny Mann, David McCauley, John McConville, Marcia McFee, Melinda McLain, Patricia Plude, Enver Rahmanov, Jonathan Relucio, Megan Shirle, Stan Stewart, Shelli Teed-Bose, Debra Weir, and especially Jonathan Leavy, our third hard flapping and singing "winger" during the crucial years of developing InterPlay.

Body Wisdom Board, playdough people, your phenomenal support made this book possible. Susanne Mulcahy, Randy Newswanger, Katharine Kunst, Annlee McGurk, Anne Sigler, Leo Keegan, Leslie Warren, Penny Mann, and Trixie Schnedar, you prove that InterPlay makes non-profit life powerful and fun.

Regional InterPlay leaders, colleagues, and playmates in our formative years, thank you for being ecstatic followers: InterPlay superstars Tom Henderson and Ginny Going, in Raleigh/Durham; Krista Harris and Ingrid Hurlen, in Seattle; Jane Siarny, in Chicago; Linda Schlabach Miller and John Glick, in Indiana; CathyAnn Beaty, Don Portwood, Maarja Roth and Becky Myrick, in Minneapolis; Sheila Collins and Rich Citrin, in Texas; Janie Oakes and Joa Datillo, in New Mexico; Rod Pattenden and Trisha Watts in Sydney, Australia; Meg MacLeod in Asheville, North Carolina; Diane Saliba Ault, in Nashville; Ellen Oak, in Boston.

My philanthropic bodyspirit advocates and friends, Johannas, Mary Ellen, Randy, Cortlandt, and Janie, true gracemakers, your play with resources makes grace multiply a billionfold.

I should not be surprised after a life lived in wide-eyed synchronicity and grace that I would find Wood Lake Publishing. Spirit led me right to you and you said yes to this book. Lois Huey-Heck, Mike Schwartzentruber and all of you who took on *Move: What the Body Wants*, I am honoured and overjoyed by working with you.

And Phil. No words. Only grace. Jumping up and down, flinging and flying, as fine as a man gets, your hands, heart, spirit, and mind are on every word in this book. Thank you for making me laugh. You are the bubba.

RESOURCES

To find Interplay near you; to learn about the InterPlay Leadership Program, "Mentoring for an Embodied Life"; to attend a "What If Life Didn't Have to be So Hard" InterPlay experience, or for other opportunities, go to **www.interplay.org**.

OTHER INTERPLAY BOOKS

HAVING IT ALL:
BODY, MIND, HEART & SPIRIT TOGETHER AGAIN AT LAST
by Phil Porter with Cynthia Winton-Henry
Advice, tools, stories, and photos
for those who want more in their lives: more grace, more community, more connection, more laughter, more ease, more integration. *Having It All* questions the ways we have learned to categorize our experience. It seeks to heal the conflicts and splits in our individual and communal lives.

DANCE: THE SACRED ART
THE JOY OF MOVEMENT AS A SPIRITUAL PRACTICE
by Cynthia Winton-Henry
If you're thinking, "But I'm not a dancer" or "I feel awkward," I hope to reassure you. You don't need a special talent to move. You don't need to be "graceful" or especially coordinated. You don't need a body that's "in shape." Dancing helps us embrace all this humanity. Dance connects us to the holy of life. – from the Introduction

CHASING THE DANCE OF LIFE: A FAITH JOURNEY
by Cynthia Winton-Henry

A memoir: What do you do if you hear voices or see things? As a Euro-American woman I'll tell you what you *should* do. You should shut up. However, if voices prod you to quench the thirst for big human needs like Love, Justice, and Freedom, you might become a blabbermouth performance artist like me. You might try to demystify dance, healing rituals and communal peacemaking enough to wave a flag in sight of the mainstream. The voice of Love is *that* compelling...

BIBLIOGRAPHY

Ackerman, Diane. *Deep Play*. New York: Random House, 1999.

Berry, Thomas. *The Great Work: Our Way into the Future*. New York: Bell Tower, 1999.

Collins, Sheila K. *Stillpoint: The Dance of Selfhealing, Selfcaring: A Playbook for People Who Do Caring Work*. Fort Worth: TLC Productions, 1992.

Csikszentmhalyi, Mihaly. *Flow: The Psychology of Optimal Experience*. New York: Quality Paperback Book Club, 2001.

Goudey, June. *The Feast of Our Lives: Reimaging Communion*. Cleveland: The Pilgrim Press, 2002.

Hammershalg, Carl A. *The Dancing Healers: A Doctor's Journey of Healing With Native Americans*. San Francisco: Harper and Row, 1989.

Horowitz, Claudia. *The Spiritual Activist: Practices to Transform Your Life, Your Work, and Your World*. New York: Penguin Compass, 2002.

Ingerman, Sandra. *Soul Retrieval: Mending the Fragmented Self*. San Francisco: HarperSanFrancisco, 1991.

Luterman, Alison. *Living the Largest Possible Life*. Cleveland: Cleveland State University Poetry Center, 2001.

McAfee Brown, Robert. *Spirituality and Liberation: Overcoming the Great Fallacy*. Philadelphia: The Westminster Press, 1988.

Miller, Kamae A. *Wisdom Comes Dancing: Selected Writings of Ruth St. Denis on Dance, Spirituality and the Body*. Seattle: PeaceWorks, 1997.

Mindell, Arne. *The Shaman's Body: A New Shamanism for Transforming Health, Relationships, and the Community.* San Francisco: Harper, 1993.

Moore, Thomas. *The Soul of Sex: Cultivating Life as an Act of Love.* New York: HarperCollinsPublishers, 1998.

Myss, Carolyn. *Anatomy of the Spirit.* New York: Harmony Books, 1996.

Nackmanovitch, Stephen. *Free Play: Improvisation in Art and Life.* Los Angeles: Jeremy P. Tarcher, 1990.

Porter, Phil, with Cynthia Winton-Henry. *Having It All: Body, Mind, Heart, and Spirit Together Again At Last.* Oakland: Wing It! Press, 1997.

Rock, Judith, and Norman Mealy. *Performer as Priest and Prophet: Restoring the Intuitive to Worship through Music and Dance.* San Francisco: HarperCollins, 1988.

Schroeder, Celeste Snowber. *Embodied Prayer: Harmonizing Body and Soul.* Kelowna, BC: Northstone Publishing, 2004.

Some, Malidoma Patrice. *The Healing Wisdom of Africa: Finding Life Purpose through Nature, Ritual, and Community.* New York: Jeremy P. Tarcher, 1999.

Some, Sobonfu. *The Spirit of Intimacy: Ancient African Teachings in the Ways of Relationships.* New York: William Morrow, 1997.

Wheatley, Margaret J., and Byron Kellner-Rogers. *A Simpler Way.* San Francisco: Berrett-Koehler Publishers, 1996.

Wuellner, Flora. *Prayer and Our Bodies.* Nashville: The Upper Room, 1987.

INDEX OF MEDITATIONS, JOURNALLING, PRACTICES, AND PLAY

HOW TO ACCESS THE *LIKE BREATHING* AUDIO FILES

To listen to or download the *Like Breathing* audio files suggested in this book, go to **www.woodlakebooks.com/movemusic** and enter the following user name and password.

Username: **inter**

Password: **play**

LIKE BREATHING TRACK LIST

All tracks copyright © 2001 Body Wisdom, Inc.
All rights reserved.

1. Body Prayer
2. Like Breathing
3. My Heart Is Open
4. Kokopele
5. Walk Stop Run
6. Strut and Jive
7. Over the Edge
8. Kyrie
9. Reflection
10. Fried Chicken
11. Play
12. Freedom
13. Release
14. On Behalf Of
15. Offering
16. Home and Away
17. Open the Door
18. Turban Blues
19. Picture This
20. What the Body Wants

WOOD LAKE

IMAGINING, LIVING, AND TELLING
THE FAITH STORY.

WOOD LAKE IS THE FAITH STORY COMPANY.

It has told

- the story of the seasons of the earth, the people of God, and the place and purpose of faith in the world;
- the story of the faith journey, from birth to death;
- the story of Jesus and the churches that carry his message.

Wood Lake has been telling stories for more than 30 years. During that time, it has given form and substance to the words, songs, pictures, and ideas of hundreds of storytellers.

Those stories have taken a multitude of forms – parables, poems, drawings, prayers, epiphanies, songs, books, paintings, hymns, curricula – all driven by a common mission of serving those on the faith journey.